Werner Steinigeweg

The New Softbill Handbook

Everything About Care, Feeding, Illnesses, and Breeding

With a Special Chapter on Understanding
Behavior and Descriptions of
Popular Species

With thirty color photographs by eminent photographers
and thirty drawings by Gertrud Thomas

Translated by Rita and Robert Kimber

American Advisor-Editor: Matthew Vriends, Ph.D.

BARRON'S

All inquiries should be addressed to:
Barron's Educational Series, Inc.
250 Wireless Boulevard
Hauppauge, NY 11788

Library of Congress Catalog Card No. 88-24149

International Standard Book No. 0-8120-4075-9

Library of Congress Cataloging-in-Publication Data

Steinigewag, Werner.

    Softbills: everything about care, feeding, illnesses, and breeding: with a special chapter on understanding behavior and descriptions of popular species / Werner Steinigewag; with 30 color photos by eminent photographers and 30 drawings by Gertrud Thomas; translated by Rita and Robert Kimber; American advisor-editor. Matthew Vriends.

    Translation of: Weichfresser.
    Bibliography
    Includes index.
    ISBN 0-8120-4075-9
    1. Softbills. I. Vriends, Matthew M., 1937– . II. Title.
SF473.S64S7413 1988
636.6'869—dc19
                    88-24149

PRINTED IN HONG KONG
3456   9927   9876543

The color photos on the covers depict
Front cover: A pair of Pekin robins
Inside front cover: An Indian (or oriental) white-eye
Inside back cover: A pair of pagoda mynahs
Back cover: Above: A mynah and a silver-eared mesia. Middle: Three Indian (or oriental) white-eyes and a red-eared bulbul. Below: A pagoda mynah and a shama.

Photo Credits
Fischer: Inside back cover; Lenz: page 45; Reinhard: pages 17 (below, right), 18, 27 (above), and 46 (below, left and right); Scholtz/H. van Os: front cover; Scholtz: inside front cover, pages 17 (below, left), 28, 46 (above), 79 (above, left, and below, left), 80, and back cover; Schrempp: page 27 (below, left and right); Wothe: pages 17 (above), and 79 (above, right and below, right).

Werner Steinigeweg
is a veterinarian and heads the Public Relations Office of the College of Veterinary Medicine in Hannover (West Germany). He has more than 20 years of experience in the aviculture of native as well as of exotic songbirds and is especially interested in some of the softbills described in this book, particularly in white-eyes. He is the author of numerous publications in specialized periodicals.

A note of warning
The subject of this book is how to take care of various songbirds (namely, softbills) in captivity. In dealing with these birds, always remember that newly purchased birds — even when they appear perfectly healthy — may well be carriers of salmonellae. This is why it is highly advisable to have sample droppings analyzed and to observe strict hygienic rules. Other infectious diseases that can endanger humans, such as ornithosis and tuberculosis, are extremely rare in songbirds. Still, if you see a doctor because you or a member of your household has symptoms of a cold or of the flu, mention that you keep birds. No one who is allergic to feathers or feather dust should keep birds. If you have any doubts, consult your physician before you buy a bird.

    Most food insects are pests that infest stored food or are a general nuisance in our households. If you decide to grow any of these insects, you should therefore be extra careful to prevent them from escaping from their containers (see page 39).

Contents

Contents

Preface

Is there anyone who doesn't know Hans Christian Andersen's fairytale about the nightingale whose "sweet song" enchanted not only the Emperor of China but even "Death himself"? The bird in this story is presumably a *Leiothrix lutea*, or Pekin robin, which belongs to a large group of exotic songbirds that feed on insects, fruit, or nectar. Because of their diet, they are called softbills by aviculturists.

Werner Steinigeweg, who is a veterinarian, a member of the staff of the Veterinary College of Hannover (West Germany), and the author of this book, has been keeping and breeding white-eyes, bulbuls, Pekin robins, and other softbills for many years. In this practical handbook he introduces 28 exotic softbills that are often kept as cage birds. The descriptions include advice on how to keep and breed each species as well as detailed information on the place of origin, appearance, behavior, and typical song of the birds.

All the softbills introduced in this handbook are wild birds. In contrast to domesticated pet birds, such as canaries, which have adapted completely to life in a man-made environment, caged wild birds retain almost all the traits and varied behavior that characterize their cousins in the wild, even if they have been cage-bred for two or three generations. This is what makes watching them so intriguing.

Softbills are considerably more demanding about diet and nesting conditions than seed-eating birds. If a pair of birds is disturbed during courtship they will not mate, and the parent birds must have insects that resemble the prey they find in nature to feed their young.

You'll be most successful in the care and breeding of your exotic birds — and able to provide conditions for them that correspond most closely to those of nature — if you read the information contained in this handbook carefully. You'll find out about different kinds of housing: regular and glass cages, indoor aviaries, and outdoor ones with a shelter. Equally useful are the tips on how to help your birds become used to their new home. The author explains when birds can or should be kept singly and when in a community, and specific questions that come up in the course of keeping and raising softbills are discussed. There is a chapter on how to recognize and treat illnesses and one filled with detailed information on basic bird foods, dietary supplements, and live food. A special chapter contains simple instructions on growing various insects to feed to the birds live.

If your birds are properly cared for and happy they are most likely to reproduce. The chapter Raising Softbills will supply you with all the necessary information on this topic.

And now a few words on the protection of endangered species: None of the birds described in this handbook is subject to national or international regulations. A number of other exotic softbills whose demands are similar to those of the species described here do come under those regulations, however. This is why this book explains what you as a bird owner should know about the protection of endangered species. The rules for bringing pet birds into the United States have also been included.

The author and the publisher would like to thank all those who have worked on the book: Gertrud Thomas for her instructive drawings; the photographers for their attractive photos; and Dr. Sigurd Raethel for checking the chapter Health Care and List of Diseases.

Considerations Before You Buy

What Is a Softbill?

The word *softbill* is not a zoological term like the word *finch*, which describes birds that are related to each other. Instead it is a term applied to various birds that belong to different genera and families but that all share one characteristic. Softbills, unlike most other cage birds, don't live on seeds. They can be subdivided according to the kind of food they prefer into the following groups:

• insectivores, which feed on insects
• frugivores, which live on fruit
• nectarivores, which drink the nectar of flowers

In most cases it is easy to tell softbills from seed eaters by the shape of the bill (see drawing). There are some subtle differences of behavior as well, however. Generally, softbills living in captivity learn to trust humans more quickly than do seed eaters.

The shape of the bill is an indicator of the kind of food a bird eats. Softbills (left) have slender bills; the bills of seed-eating birds (right) are thicker and conical.

Note: The softbills described in this handbook — with the exception of the Muscicapidae, or flycatchers (see page 71), which live almost exclusively on insects — eat more than one kind of food, with individual preferences that vary from species to species.

What Is Involved in Keeping Softbills?

Before you go out to buy a softbill you should ask yourself seriously whether these birds fit into your way of life. Each species has specific demands that must be met if the birds are to be happy and healthy and give you years of pleasure.

Daily Care: Bird owners can't take any days off. Every day some time has to be set aside for the birds, not only for feeding them and cleaning the cage or aviary, but also for getting and taking care of live food. Before vacations and in case of sickness, plans have to be made to ensure that the birds get their daily care (see page 7).

Live Food: Feeding live insects to birds is not everybody's cup of tea, but it is necessary if you want your softbills to have something to eat that resembles what they would get in the wild. If you hate insects, or if you feel sorry for them because they have to be killed, you should not keep softbilled birds.

Sharing Your Living Space: If you plan to keep birds indoors you should keep in mind the following:

• You'll have to spend more time cleaning house, because unless you keep your birds in a glass cage, the birds' movements will send feathers and stirred-up dust flying through the grating of the cage or aviary. When the birds are flying around in the room, they leave soft droppings that are not as easy to clean up as the droppings of seed eaters. If you don't clean your softbills' quarters frequently enough, the smell can become a problem.

• When birds move in with you, so do constant activity and noise. You can't turn off a singing bird like a radio. Some excessively sensitive people are irritated by the mere sound of a bird hopping around in its cage.

• Remember about allergies! If you or a member of your family is allergic to feather dust, you cannot keep birds. If you are at all in doubt, consult your physician.

Living Conditions: It takes time before a softbill begins to trust you. Remember that these birds are basically wild creatures and can't be taught to adjust to human living conditions the same way a parakeet or a dog can. Birds are not cuddly animals and hate to be touched under normal circumstances; the most you can hope for is that they hop onto your hand to get a favorite treat.

Softbills need a quiet spot for their cage and a regular daily routine. Being in the same room with people smoking, lots of visitors, noisy children, or a television kept on late into the night all interfere with their well-being.

Softbills and Children

Softbills are not good pets for small children who like to establish closeness to animals through physical contact. The mere presence of children playing near the cage can be upsetting to the birds.

Older children with more understanding and an interest in bird behavior can have a lot of fun watching the birds. Parents should introduce their children gently and with a constant watchful eye to the tasks of feeding and looking after the birds. If done properly, this can become an important educational experience and can awaken in a child a sensitivity for our natural environment and its living creatures.

Softbills and Other Pets

Dogs and cats are natural hunters, which is why you should never let your birds fly free in the same room with them, even after the two pets are accustomed to each other. Even safely locked in a cage, these birds are best not left alone in a room with a cat or dog because great anxiety or a state of panic may be enough to cause death.

Climbing rodents (chipmunks, for example) may also cause panic or may try to bite at the birds between the bars of the cage.

Vacation Care

Even acclimated birds suffer when there are changes in their environment or when their normal life rhythm is disrupted. This is why you should try to leave them in their accustomed surroundings, if at all possible, and ask a reliable person to look after them. Ideally, you should entrust the care of your birds to an experienced bird fancier because such a person knows how to deal with any problems (such as illness) that might come up and will not worry needlessly or get upset over normal occurrences, such as molting or regurgitating bits of feathers.

If you keep your birds in an aviary, you have no choice but to arrange for a caretaker.

A single bird (or two, or three) can often be boarded at the pet shop where it was bought. If you plan to transport the bird in a small travel cage, substitute this cage for the bird's regular quarters several days ahead so that the smaller cage feels like home when it's time for the journey.

Note: A mynah that has become attached to its human companions should spend the vacation with another family — it will suffer less from loneliness.

Should You Keep Birds Singly or in Pairs?

There is no simple answer to this question. Some softbills, like the white-eyes, are sociable and get along well in an aviary, even if combined with birds of different species. Others, such as Shamas, are complete loners. The table briefly summarizes the major traits of the softbills commonly kept as pets. For more detailed information, turn to the descriptions starting on page 68. Deviations from a species' normal behavior are not uncommon.

A single bird generally becomes tame more quickly than one that lives in a community of birds. If you decide to keep a naturally gregarious softbill — that is, one of a species that lives in flocks in the wild — in a cage all by itself, the bird will depend on you for companionship. You will have to devote time and affection to it to make up for the absence of an avian partner — not just now and then, but for several hours every day.

Considerations Before You Buy

Characteristics of Various Kinds of Softbills

Since softbills vary significantly not only in appearance and song but also in behavior and demands, you should find out as much as you can about the species you are interested in before you buy a bird. Facts about the feeding requirements, typical vocalizations and social behavoir of representative species are summarized in the chart below. For facts about breeding and additional information on a variety of popular softbills, see pages 68–95.

Summary of the Different Species

Species	Diet	Voice	Compatibility
Pekin Robin	Insects, fruit	Musical, loud song but rather monotonous	Sociable; compatible even with smaller birds; should be kept in pairs
Shamas	Insects	Varied, melodious song; great talent for mocking; females sing too	Loner with distinctly territorial behavoir; only one bird per cage; pairs must be introduced to each other slowly in an aviary
White-eyes	Fruit, nectar, insects	Soft, pleasant song	Get along well with others expect when a settled pair is housed together with other birds of the same species
Gold-fronted Leafbird	Nectar, fruit, insects	Varied and vigorous song; talent for imitating	Very belligerent, especially toward its own kind and related species; even combining a pair is difficult
Red-eared Bulbul	Fruits, insects	Musical calls but no real clear song	Peaceful, but often causes confusion in an aviary because of its wild behavior; pairs very aggressive toward birds of same or related species; eventually becomes very tame if kept singly, but should be kept in pairs
Mynah	Fruits, insects	Loud(!) calls, exceptional talent for mimicking (good talker)	Very sociable but is usually kept singly; it then becomes very tame but requries much time and attention

Advice for Buying Birds

Where To Find Softbills

Pet Dealers: Most people buy their softbills at a pet shop. This has a number of advantages. You can choose the bird you like, and while you watch it in the store you have a chance to assess its state of health as well as observe the conditions under which it has been living. In most cases the trip home from the store is short and therefore not too much of a strain for the bird. If problems arise during acclimation or later, you can turn to the pet dealer for advice that is generally well-informed. Most pet stores have only a limited selection of softbills, however, and if you can't find the kind of bird there that you are looking for you must turn to other sources.

A bathing mynah. Mynahs love to play in the water. Water is splashed all over in the process, so the birdbath should be on the floor and away from furniture.

Note: When buying a softbill, be sure to find out if it belongs to a protected species (see Protection of Endangered Species, page 68). If you acquire a bird on the endangered list, you must adhere strictly to any prescribed regulations.

Mail-order Dealers: You can order softbills from a catalog, and they will be shipped to you. This method has serious disadvantages, however. First, you know nothing about the bird's state of health or previous history. Second, shipping is likely to take many hours and may expose the bird to considerable temperature changes, which is stressful for the bird. Because softbills are relatively rare, on the other hand, buying through the mail may be the only way to obtain a bird of a certain species and of the desired sex.

Note: If you consider going this route, ask experienced bird fanciers or aviculturists for the names of reputable mail-order suppliers who deal only in carefully acclimated and healthy birds and take special care in handling and shipping them.

Breeders: A breeder will sell you a well-acclimated bird that is used to human care and to a diet you can easily duplicate. Since breeding softbills is not yet common, however, purchase from a breeder is still the exception rather than the rule. A good way to find and get in touch with breeders is to contact some of the bird clubs listed on page 96.

Periodicals: Bird magazines (see Addresses, page 96) often have a classified section where softbills may be offered for sale. In these advertisements, a kind of shorthand with numbers is often used to indicate how many birds of which sex are available. Thus, "1,2" means one male and two females; "0,3" means three females. As a lover of birds, you want to pick up the birds yourself from the person selling them. This way you not only get to see how the birds have been kept, but you also spare the birds the hardship of being shipped.

How to Tell a Healthy Bird from a Sick One

Not every sickness is apparent at first glance. There are some signs that can help you assess a bird's state of health, however. If you are a novice in the field of aviculture, it is best to invite along a knowledgeable bird fancier when you go shopping for a bird so that you pick the right one.

First, have a good look at the bird's environment. The food and water should be fresh, and the

Advice For Buying Birds

A pair of Pekin robins sitting side by side. Even when flying freely in the room, the partners periodically stop to sit nestled together.

cage should be clean, not overcrowded.

Then observe the bird or group of birds you are interested in for a while. If there are several birds of the same kind in the cage, note individual differences in coloring or missing feathers so that you'll be able to recognize the bird of your choice when it's time to remove it from the cage.

Behavior: A healthy bird is vivacious, interacts with the other birds, and takes a lively interest in its surroundings. Display of fear is not a negative sign in a wild bird—on the contrary. A bird that sits apathetically on its perch and lets you approach or reach for it without shying away is almost invariably sick. Even a tame bird does not let you take it in your hand without struggling. Sick birds often sit in front of their food dishes with puffed-up feathers and poke around listlessly in the food without really eating.

Plumage: The feathers of a healthy bird hug the body smoothly; ruffled or ragged plumage or feathers stuck together near the vent are signs of illness. Bare spots and broken tail or flight feathers, however, are usually caused by nothing more serious than transport or crowded quarters. Feathers that were pulled out grow back within a few days in a healthy bird, and large mangled feathers are replaced by new ones in the next molt.

Feet: The feet should be smooth and clean, without excessive growth of the horny scales (see drawing on page 58), without inflammations or sores, and without overgrown nails (see drawing on page 14). Foot problems are very hard to cure in birds. Ask to have a very close look at the feet after the softbill of your choice has been removed from the cage.

State of Nutrition: While the salesperson is holding the bird, check how well nourished it is. You should feel the strong breast muscles, and the sternum should never protrude sharply. The abdomen is slightly hollow in a bird that is in good physical shape. A small fat cushion is not tragic, but if you can see or feel that the intestines are stuffed, this is a sign of serious internal disease.

Housing

The cage or aviary should provide an environment for your softbills in which they feel secure and happy. This is why it is so important to set it up in such a way that
• it meets the birds' needs and allows for their natural way of life
• it can be cleaned easily
• it is pleasant to look at for the observer

If your softbills' home meets these tests, the birds are content to return to it even after flying free in the room.

The Right Spot

When deciding where to place the cage or aviary, you will no doubt start out with your own wishes and the givens of the available space. You must also take into account the birds' sensibilities, however, for even minor changes and distur-

bances near the cage can give rise to fear and nervousness.

The Right Cage

For a single softbill, a cage is the least expensive and easiest form of housing, but it represents a severe limitation of movement.

You need a cage in any case even if you have a bird room or an aviary for several softbills. A cage is required
• for introducing new birds into the community
• for quarantining sick birds (see page 54)
• as temporary quarters for competing birds (as during the mating season)
• as a living space for the softbills while you renovate their aviary

Pet stores offer a wide variety of cages that are suitable for softbills. When you make your choice, keep the following criteria in mind.

Size: A bird cage can never be too large. At the very least, the inhabitant must be able to use its wings when hopping from perch to perch. The length of the cage is what matters; height is not so crucial. If your softbill is able to fly freely in the room every day, a cage with the minimum measurements given in the table on page 12 is adequate. These measurements should be increased as much as possible if your softbill has little opportunity for free flying or if you keep several birds in one cage.

Note: The wire cages commonly sold for canaries and parakeets are too small for softbills.

Shape: The cage of a softbill should be a simple rectangular space, without balconies, turrets, or other embellishments. Unnecessary ornamentation only interferes with the bird's freedom of movement and may cause injuries. The floor area should be rectangular, with the wide side facing front rather than being sideways so that the bird can move to one side when you have to reach into the cage. Round cages should be avoided.

Guidelines for Placement of a Bird Cage

Needs of the birds	Recommended location
Stable conditions; absence of upsetting events (children, other pets!); undisturbed rest at night	A quiet spot at human eye level, not near a TV set
Shelter and protection	Not exposed on all sides; next to a wall or in a corner
Fresh air (but no drafts!)	Near a window
Light; also sufficient daylight (12 to 14 hours)	Near a window, or supply artificial light (see page 21)

Housing

Minimum Measurements for Cages

(Width × depth × height; approximate measurements)

Species	Single bird	Pairs
White-eyes	Not possible	24 × 12 × 20 inches (60 × 30 × 50 cm)
Pekin robin	Not advisable	32 × 20 × 20 inches (80 × 50 × 50 cm)
Leafbirds	24 × 16 × 24 inches (60 × 40 × 60 cm)	Only in an aviary
Bulbuls	Not advisable	32 × 20 × 20 inches (80 × 50 × 50 cm)
Shamas	24 × 16 × 24 inches (60 × 40 × 60 cm)	Only in fairly large aviaries
Mynahs	32 × 20 × 20 inches (80 × 50 × 50 cm)	Only in fairly large aviaries

Wire Cages

A wire cage is made up of metal bars with a plastic pan at the bottom that has a built-in clean-out drawer. These cages are easy to maintain and hygienic. Cages that lack the clean-out drawer are more complicated to clean and therefore not as practical for softbills, whose litter has to be changed frequently.

Cage Bars: A cage for softbills should have vertical bars on at least two sides. Unlike parrots, which like to climb, softbills can grip vertical bars better than horizontal bars. The bars should not be set too far apart — the exact spacing depends on the size of the birds — or the birds can stick their heads between the bars and possibly strangle themselves.

Note: The bars should be chrome plated or plastic covered. Cages made of copper or brass can cause poisoning if verdigris forms on the metal.

Doors: The more doors a cage has, the better. If there are several doors, you can reach into all areas of the cage interior without difficulty. A recommended design has two doors in the front and one on each side.

Box Cages

Pet stores often label box cages as softbill cages because they are particularly practical for this type of bird. In box cages, the floor, top, back, and sides are made of wood or some kind of synthetic material, and the front consists of bars or a combination of bars and glass (see drawing on page 13). Since only one side is open, much less dirt is generated than in a wire cage that has bars on all sides. In addition, a box cage gives softbills — birds that in nature live among dense bushes — more of a sense of protection and safety.

Tips for building a cage yourself: Plastic-coated plywood is a good building material for this purpose; ⅜ inch (9 mm) plywood is thick enough for cages up to 3 feet (1 m) long. For painting the interior, white is a practical color; it makes the space brighter for the birds, and the softbills are easier to see against a white background. Pet supply stores sell ready-made front panels with doors already built in. If you build the front panel yourself, stretch plastic-covered wire mesh over a wood frame. Don't forget the doors! Plastic clean-out drawers may be available at a pet supply store; sheet metal drawers can be custom built by a tinsmith; or you can build your own out of wood (but wood requires more maintenance!).

Build with as few seams as possible; cracks make perfect hiding places for ectoparasites, such as mites, and are hard to disinfect. Cover any exposed wood with a coat of varnish.

Glass Cages

A glass cage is just like a box cage except that it has a glass front and the doors are located on the sides. The sides also have slits or grating that serve as vents. For safety's sake you should have a spare glass panel on hand in case the glass front breaks.

Advantages:
• It is easier to see a bird without the visual interference of bars.
• The dirt doesn't fly out into the room.
• If you cover the vents with window screening you can feed the birds live insects.

Disadvantages:
• A glass cage takes more time to keep clean. When glass gets dirty, which it does quickly, it looks terrible. Therefore it must be cleaned often.
• Shy birds often feel less safe behind glass and flutter around nervously at the slightest disturbance.
• The glass acts as a barrier, and it takes softbills longer to establish contact with their caretaker; many birds never overcome their timidity as long as they live in a glass cage.
• Insufficient air exchange can give rise to hygienic problems.

A terrarium cage is a glass cage with lots of vegetation growing in it. It represents an attempt to create a space that resembles the birds' natural environment. But there are drawbacks! A terrarium cage requires a great deal of maintenance. The plants soon become unattractive because of bird droppings and bite marks. Also, the birds can pick up intestinal parasites and fungi from the soil in which the plants are growing. A better solution is to have lots of plants near the cage. The birds can then play in them when they fly freely in the room.

An Indoor Aviary

In pet stores, large cages are often labeled "indoor aviaries." We mean by this term a space that allows the birds to really fly for a short distance. This requires dimensions of about 72 × 36 × 36 inches (200 × 100 × 100 cm). Such generous quarters well suit the natural needs of softbills. Having more space allows the birds to be more active, and just as in humans, increased physical activity means a healthier metabolism, making the birds less prone to obesity and keeping them fitter. For this reason indoor aviaries are highly recommended for softbills, even if you keep only one bird or a single pair.

The pet trade offers a wide assortment of indoor aviaries, either completely finished or as kits of prefabricated parts that you can assemble to suit your own taste. If you are handy with tools, you can

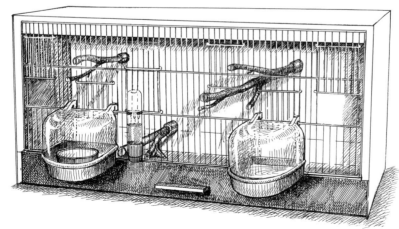

A box cage is particularly useful for housing softbills. Important features and accessories are a clean-out drawer, several doors, bathhouses for bathing and for food, a water dispenser, and some branches. Mountings in the wall make it easy to exchange the branches.

build an aviary from scratch to fit the space you have. Keep in mind the following:

• The aviary must be deep enough to allow your softbills to fly properly.

• All parts of the aviary must be accessible; access can be provided through one large door or several smaller ones or through a removable side panel.

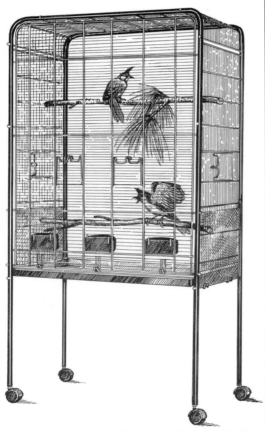

A small indoor aviary: If the aviary is equipped with casters, you can easily move it to the balcony or terrace when the weather is sunny. The birds depicted in this aviary are red-eared bulbuls.

Setting up a Cage or Indoor Aviary

Perches

Good perches are crucial for healthy legs and feet. Softbills should have natural branches to perch on. Commercially available perches made of hardwood or plastic are recommended for a quarantine cage only (see page 54). If they are used all the time, your birds are likely to develop joint problems and sore spots on the soles of their feet because these perches don't have any spring to them when a bird lands on them, and their uniform diameter and the usual parallel placement results in an uneven strain on the legs and feet.

Natural branches, on the other hand, are flexible if mounted properly and force the feet to adjust constantly to their irregular shape. The rough surface provides wear for the claws. Good sources of branches are fruit trees (unsprayed!) and other deciduous trees, such as birches, willows, and elderberry bushes. Never gather branches along the roadside because of the residue from car exhaust!

The diameter of the branches should be large enough that the bird's toes don't quite reach around (see drawing). This way the nails are worn down properly and there is no need for nail trimming.

The diameter of the perches should be big enough that the bird's toes can almost but not quite reach around the perch. This way the claws get enough wear. Left: A perch of the correct thickness. Right: A perch that is too thin.

Arrangement: Don't crowd a cage or aviary with branches at the expense of flying space. The lower branches should be placed away from higher perches so that they are safe from droppings from above. This saves your having to change them all the time. Softbills like to sleep in the upper part of the cage. If you have several birds, you must be sure there are enough sleeping perches.

Housing

Mounting perches: Different mounting methods suit various cage types.

Pet stores sell special mountings for attaching branches to a wire cage, or you can tie the branches to the bars with wire.

Box or glass cages usually come with mountings to hold perches or branches, or you can install brackets for this purpose yourself. The branches are stuck into these brackets and are then easy to replace. Another possibility is to hang the branches on wires tied to hook eyes that are screwed into the cage roof or walls. The wires also help reduce the noise of birds hopping on and off the perches, which is annoyingly loud if the branches are in direct contact with the cage because the cage acts as a sounding board.

Branches are mounted the same way in an indoor aviary as in a cage.

Food Dishes

Pet stores sell many different kinds of plastic and ceramic food dishes. The best kind to pick are glazed ceramic or glass dishes. They are heavy enough not to tip over when the birds perch on the rim, which they like to do when eating. The optimal shape is a round, shallow bowl — round because a round bowl is easier to clean than a dish with corners, and shallow because the birds can pick what they like better if the food is spread out. However, live insects should be offered in a deeper bowl with smooth, dry sides so that the larvae cannot crawl out.

Water Dishes

Softbills need fresh water daily. Automatic waterers are best because the water stays cleaner in them than in an open bowl.

There are special nectar dispensers made of dark glass. They are equipped with a nipple, from which the birds imbibe the liquid with their brushlike tongues (see drawing on page 22). The dark glass helps to preserve the added nutrients, some of which (many vitamins, for instance) quickly deteriorate if exposed to direct light. The beaks of most softbills are shorter and stronger than those of hummingbirds and other nectar-drinking birds for which these dispensers are designed. Therefore be sure to pick a dispenser with a nipple that is short and wide enough.

Note: Always assemble the dispensers carefully, and check every day that they are working properly so that the liquid does not leak out.

Placement of Food and Water Dishes

It is important that food and water not be contaminated with droppings, bathwater, or sand. If you set the food dishes into (dry!) bathhouses inside a cage or indoor aviary (see drawing on page 13), the food stays clean and you need not reach into the cage when putting out fresh food. This arrangement spares nervous birds many anxious moments.

A Place for Bathing

All softbills like to take baths. Since the birds use the bathwater not just for bathing but also for drinking, however, the birdbath must be cleaned daily and fresh water supplied.

A bathhouse: Choose a bathhouse that can be disassembled for cleaning. Open water basins are not practical in a cage or indoor aviary because the birds love to splash and get everything wet and also because leftover food, droppings, and sand can contaminate the water and turn it into a breeding ground for bacteria.

Placement: For birds like shamas, which like bathing on the ground, the birdbath should be placed on the floor of the cage (see drawing on page 9). Tree dwellers like leafbirds, white-eyes, and bulbuls, on the other hand, prefer higher bathing sites.

The Floor Covering

The birds' excretions collect on the floor, where the birds walk and hop around and look for food.

15

Since the droppings of softbills are often quite wet, especially if the diet includes a lot of fruit and nectar, the floor covering must be changed more often than for seed eaters to prevent a bad smell and the growth of bacteria.

A good floor covering should be dust free, absorbent, and easy on the feet, and if it is used for terrestrial birds it should contain pebbles, moss cushions, dry leaves, tree bark, and similar material.

Bird sand: This is absorbent enough for softbills only if supplied in a thick layer.

Cat litter: The dust in cat litter is bad for the birds' respiratory organs. Cat litter is very absorbent, however, and therefore useful for frugivorous softbills that rarely spend time on the floor (leafbirds and white-eyes); it is not recommended for terrestrial birds like the shama.

Forest soil: This soil is a valuable source of minerals and small invertebrates, but if it's wet it can breed harmful microorganisms and if it's too dry it is very dusty. It is better to supply forest soil or small pieces of sod separately in flat containers.

Blotting paper, paper towel, etc.: These materials are highly absorbent. They must be changed daily, but this is not a great chore and allows regular inspection of the droppings.

A Bird Room and How to Set It up

The ideal solution is to give the softbills a room of their own. Such a bird room can either be set up as one large flight area or subdivided into several smaller aviaries. When preparing a bird room there are some general rules to observe.

Walls: Paint the walls with latex paint or cover them with tiles. Don't use wallpaper because it is hard to keep clean, the birds nibble on it, and vermin can hide under it.

Branches and plants: Restrict these to specific areas so that the rest of the room is open for flight and for observation. Choose and fasten the branches the same way you would for a cage or indoor aviary (see page 14).

Food and Water Dishes: Dishes should be impossible to tip over and easy to clean. They should be placed to accommodate the birds' feeding habits (see Setting up a Cage or Indoor Aviary, page 14).

A Birdbath: If the bird room is divided into smaller aviaries it is better to use bathhouses (see drawing on page 13). In an undivided room shallow bowls are ideal. Birds prefer them, they hold more water, and splashing is no problem. Remember not to set an open birdbath under perches and branches where droppings can contaminate the water.

Floor Covering: Linoleum (any seams must be absolutely tight) or tiles are easiest to clean. The floor must be wet mopped twice a week. Litter (see page 16) is not spread over the entire floor area but contained in boxes underneath the branches where the birds perch. This makes it easy to change the litter.

Special Protective Measures: Be sure there are solidly mounted screens on all windows. With the screens in place the room can be aired and exposed to direct sunlight without fear of any birds escaping. The door should have a small antechamber to trap birds that may flit out as you enter.

An Outdoor Aviary

You don't have to have a large garden to give your birds an opportunity to live outdoors; an outdoor aviary of somewhat more modest proportions can be housed on a balcony or deck. Birds love to be in the fresh air at least part of the year, and if

Starlings.
Above: An especially colorful starling, the African superb glossy starling (*Lamprospreo superbus*). Below, left: A mynah (*Gracula religiosa*). Below, right: A splendid glossy starling (*Lamprotornis splendidus*).

Housing

you hope to breed them, the chances for success are best in an outdoor aviary.

Setting up an Outdoor Aviary: Several manufacturers make prefabricated sections that can be assembled into an outdoor aviary. (Ask your pet dealer for specific suggestions.) The following rules are important to note, whether you buy an aviary or build it yourself.

Size: No quarters can be too big for softbills. It's important, however, that every last corner be accessible to you because all parts must be kept clean and you may at some point have to catch a bird.

Location: The aviary should have at least a few hours of direct sunshine. An eastern or western exposure is best; if the aviary faces south, enough shade must be provided (in the form of plants or a section of roofing). An aviary facing north is not desirable for softbills.

Foundation: If you dig a foundation for an aviary in a garden, it must be at least 3 feet (1 m) deep to keep mice and rats from burrowing in. A better solution is to pour a concrete floor with drainage for the rainwater. There is no need for a foundation if the aviary is designed for a balcony.

Frame: A frame can be made of wood or metal; in either case it must be stable and strong enough to hold up under heavy snow and to withstand windstorms.

Grating: Use plastic-covered wire mesh fine enough that the birds cannot slip through. Two layers of mesh ensure added protection against the intrusion of predators (cats, martens, sparrow hawks, and owls). The two layers of mesh should be 2 inches (5 cm) apart.

Protection against wind and weather: This is

achieved by roofing over part of the aviary. Corrugated plexiglass is a good roofing material. A partial roof offers protection from rain but doesn't eliminate rain baths for birds and plants.

In addition, provide wind protection on at least one side, or attach the aviary to the wall of a building (see drawing) so that the birds are not exposed to wind blowing through.

Setting up the Interior

There is room for creativity in shaping the space of an outdoor aviary (through planting various types of vegetation). Remember, however, that many of the objects used by the birds (food dishes and bathing basins) must not be exposed to sun and rain.

Perches: The same considerations apply as in setting up a cage (see page 14). If many plants are growing in the aviary, not many additional branches are necessary. Don't place branches in the upper third of the aviary in the section that has no roof. You don't want to encourage your softbills to sleep where they can be rained on and where cats and owls might attack them.

Food and water dishes: Offer shamas and their relatives their food in special spots on the ground; for arboreal birds (leafbirds, white-eyes, and bulbuls), display the food on a small stand or platform. Food and water dishes belong in the section of the aviary that is roofed over to prevent soaking and contamination (e.g., through the droppings of wild birds). Make sure no perches are located above the feeding stations.

Birdbaths: If your softbills live outdoors you can let them play in the water to their heart's content. There is no need for an enclosed bathhouse. Good-sized, shallow, and sturdy bowls (make sure they contain no asbestos) are practical. For terrestrial birds the bowls should not stand on the bare soil or sand (danger of harmful bacteria) but should be placed on tiles or flagstones, or at least on coarse gravel. Tree-dwellers prefer taking baths higher up.

Chestnut-flanked white-eye (*Zosterops erythropleurus*) with bleached plumage. The head, nape, and back should be olive green, but under improper conditions this original color can quickly fade to gray.

19

Housing

The bathing sites should always be in the covered area of the aviary.

The Floor

For an aviary on a balcony or deck, a floor of cement tiles is best. Such a floor can be hosed down easily if it has a drain, and it dries quickly after a shower.

In an aviary built outdoors, the floor usually consists of earth or sand. Unfortunately this is a breeding ground for pathogens, and regular care of the ground is particularly important.

Plants

Use plants growing in buckets for an aviary set up on a balcony or deck.

In a garden aviary, the plants are set in the ground. The density of the vegetation should reflect the natural habitat of the particular softbills you have, but you should always be able to reach all areas of the aviary and be able to cultivate the ground. Also, keep the vegetation from intruding on the flying space and from obstructing your view. Suitable plants are deciduous and evergreen trees or bushes like elderberry and scrub pine (no bushes with thorns). Choose plants that attract insects; those native to your area are especially suitable. Plants with twiggy branches help make nest building easier for your birds, and a dense ground cover (as of ferns) is important for protecting the female during courtship, particularly in species like the shamas in which the male is known to be impetuous in the pursuit of the female.

A Birdhouse

An ideal situation exists if the outdoor aviary is attached to a heatable shelter to which the birds can retreat at any time. This is very advantageous for

An outdoor aviary connected to a birdhouse. The section on the left is roofed over to provide shelter against rain and hot sun, and the entry on the right has a small antechamber to prevent birds from escaping when their caretaker enters the aviary. Some dense vegetation offers plenty of cover to hide in and serves as a refuge for the female during courtship displays that can be quite violent with some softbills (shamas for instance).

wintering birds over (see page 26).

If your outdoor aviary is subdivided, the shelter should be split into the same number of individual spaces. The shelter can be part of your house, or you can convert a garage that is not otherwise used. A special birdhouse, constructed with the birds' needs in mind, is of course best and can also provide space for raising live food for the birds (see page 39).

A birdhouse is built and set up along the same principles as an aviary or a bird room. Make sure there is enough light (several windows or a plexiglass skylight). You can find more technical information in specialized literature (see page 96).

Technical Accessories for Cages and Aviaries

Lighting

In their native environment, the softbills of Southeast Asia have 12 to 14 hours of daylight during most of the year. They need days of similar length in captivity in order to eat enough. Since daylight also influences the functioning of hormones, an excess as well as a shortage of daylight can affect the birds negatively. Depending on the location of the cage or indoor aviary, you may have to supply artificial light — if only for a few hours a day — at least during the winter.

Lengthening the day: For this purpose you can use conventional incandescent or fluorescent lights. The lamps are set up outside the cage (but close to it); in an aviary they can be located outside or inside; if inside, they must be behind a protective grating. Incandescent bulbs also generate heat, which adds to the birds' comfort. Sometimes softbills even "sunbathe" underneath a lamp.

A substitute for daylight: Artificial light is a must if a cage or indoor aviary is set up in a dark space like a cellar or an attic. In this case you must provide not only adequate amounts of light but also the right kind with enough ultraviolet rays. Vita-lite tubes are one recommended brand. The lamps should be placed so that the birds can always get away from the light; dense plant growth is helpful for providing shade.

Note: Never use tanning lamps; the massive doses of ultraviolet rays emitted by these lamps would harm the birds' health.

Regulating the light: Since most softbills don't return to their nests until dusk, the lights should not go off suddenly. Either switch to a softer light at the end of the day or reduce the brightness with a dimmer switch. It is also advisable to leave a nightlight on throughout the night (a 15-watt bulb, for instance) so that the birds can orient themselves at all times. In total darkness they panic easily, particularly if several birds are housed together.

Note: Your birds appreciate it if you use an automatic timer for turning on and off the light because they like a predictable schedule.

Heating

Birds are comfortable at our customary indoor temperatures. In the winter they prefer humid, moderately warm (65–68°F; 18–20°C) air to the warmer dry air of central heating. (Put a pan of water on the radiator.)

Birds in an outdoor aviary or a birdhouse: The temperature in an outdoor shelter or birdhouse should be about 59 to 65° F (15–18°C) during the winter. Electric heaters or central heating is better than stoves, which are harder to regulate and use up oxygen.

Birds like to luxuriate in the rays of infrared heat lamps, but these lamps are inadequate as a sole source of heat because the warmth that they provide is too localized.

Acclimation and Care

The Trip Home

The trip home with your new softbill should be as quick and efficient as possible. For short distances (up to no more than 2 or 3 hours) cardboard boxes with air holes on one side are adequate. Birds can manage without food and water for such a short period. If you have to drive several hours, however, it is better to transport a softbill in a small cage with some food and water. Cover the cage with a light cloth to spare the bird the upsetting experience of watching an unfamiliar world flit by.

Getting Used to the New Home

When you arrive home with the bird, the cage or aviary should be ready and set up in its permanent location, with enough food and water for the first day. Having a place to bathe and some special treats helps make the transition easier. Transfer the bird into its new quarters without touching it, and make sure all windows are shut and curtains drawn before you attempt the transfer. Then leave the newcomer alone for a while so that it can calm down and get its bearings in the new surroundings. Don't show it off to strangers during the first few days. Shamas and gold-fronted leafbirds often appear calm after a surprisingly short time and may begin singing as early as the same evening or the next morning.

Note: Cover the front of a glass cage with wire mesh or a light curtain at first so that the bird will learn to think of the glass as a solid barrier. Your softbill will also feel less threatened by humans behind this visible separation from them. Don't remove the mesh or curtain all at once but in stages.

Health Care During the First Few Days

Softbills sometimes suffer from intestinal infections, primarily coccidiosis and salmonellosis, without being visibly sick (see Health Care and List of Diseases, page 54). You can check on your bird's health by taking a fecal sample to the veterinarian for analysis. Do this in the first few days, especially if the bird is going to live in a communal aviary. Then you won't have to worry about the newcomer infecting the established birds with some disease.

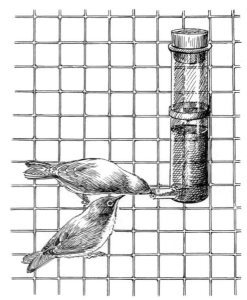

White-eyes at the drinking fountain. Birds that live on nectar (such as white-eyes and leafbirds) need a place near the nectar dispenser to perch. Unlike hummingbirds, they are unable to hover in the air while drinking.

Even with a clean bill of health from the vet, the bird cannot simply be let loose in the aviary without some forethought because the sudden introduction of a new bird can give rise to serious conflicts (see pages 8 and 65). Make sure to let the newcomer and the established birds get acquainted first, perhaps by moving their cages gradually closer or by having the birds fly freely together in the same room.

The Right Food for the First Few Days

Feed your new softbill the things it is used to for the first few days. Then you can gradually shift to the diet you plan to give it.

Caution: If the transition is too sudden, intestinal problems may result.

Refrain from giving mineral and vitamin supplements during the first few days because softbills often react badly to them. Live insects should also be used sparingly at first. Since most softbills are caught in the wild, they have probably been eating a substitute diet for a relatively short time. If they get too many insects now, they may go back to their old ways and lose their appetite for other types of food. Then you have to go through the whole process of getting them used to a new diet all over again.

Tips for Keeping Single Birds

If you decide to keep only one softbill you should choose an unsocial type of bird, perhaps a shama or a leafbird. Gregarious birds, like bulbuls and Pekin robins, need a great deal of attention from human beings to make up for the lack of avian companions.

Building Trust

Patience and special treats are the key elements in developing a relationship of trust between you and your softbill. Bother the bird as little as possible during the first few days. Limit your contact to the daily feeding and changing of the water; make no sudden or hasty moves, but talk soothingly to the bird while you perform these tasks. After a few days you can begin to hold out treats on your open hand (mealworms are very popular). Give the daily ration in small doses spread out over the entire day, and the bird soon comes to recognize and accept you as the source of this favorite food.

Daily Dealings

Once your softbill feels comfortable in its new home, has lost its fear of your hand, and finds its

A gold-fronted leafbird usually loses its shyness quickly and will hop onto your hand to get a favorite treat, such as a mealworm.

way back to the cage easily, a daily routine can be established. In addition to the necessary regular care (see page 25), this routine includes a daily free-flying session for birds that are kept in a cage. Keep in mind that exercise is essential for a bird's health and also that it is an important source of pleasure. Talk to your bird while it is flying freely — as you do when feeding it — and occasionally give it a treat. A treat also makes the return to the cage more attractive. A shama appreciates a mealworm, but a gold-fronted leafbird may be more interested in a piece of sweet fruit.

Note: Draw all the curtains in the room where the bird will fly freely to avoid fatal collisions with a window or glass door.

Does a Softbill Need Singing Lessons?

If you buy a young bird that was bred in captivity, it may not yet have mastered its whole repertoire of inherited song. In such a case you should get a record or tape with the voices and songs of your softbill's species and let your bird listen to it.

Most imported birds were caught when fully

Acclimation and Care

grown and have completed their musical training. Mocking birds like shamas and leafbirds enjoy imitating sounds and will incorporate the voices of other birds they are exposed to into their songs. Often other sounds (like radio music, the noise of a vacuum cleaner, or the humming of a hair drier) will motivate the birds to sing.

If your softbill shows little inclination to sing, you should review its diet and living conditions. Birds that are kept in pairs or in a community aviary usually sing less than single birds. Obese birds are also reluctant to sing.

In contrast to many of our native birds, birds from warmer climates sing almost year-round.

Note: If you use a tape or record, play only a few songs at a time but play them often so that your bird can learn them well.

Tips for Setting up a Community

Birds of the same species: Combine only pairs because conflicts are bound to arise in a flock of birds (even among highly social softbills) as soon as a pair has formed. Extra males are perceived as rivals and attacked by the paired birds. Vicious fights are common (see page 8), especially during the mating season.

Mixed species: Conflicts can also arise in communities including different species. They can be largely avoided, however, if
• species with different food tastes are combined (no fights over food!)
• you choose species that prefer different environments (no competition for the same space!); for example, bulbuls, leafbirds, and white-eyes spend most of their time in the upper third of the aviary; Pekin robins like the middle and the ground; shamas and dama thrushes are happiest close to the ground
• you keep birds of approximately the same size and strength together; thus, white-eyes get along well with exotic finches, Pekin robins or bulbuls are a

better match for native finches, and mynahs could be combined with pheasants

Size of the space: If you keep a flock of birds, you must have a large aviary for them. This is a prerequisite for peaceful coexistence. Crowding creates conflict.

Plenty of feeding stations: To make sure that the weaker birds, too, get to eat as much as they need, set up enough feeding stations in places that the different species naturally frequent.

Plenty of sleeping sites: Softbills like to sleep on high branches. If not enough suitable spots are available, there will be squabbling every night over who gets to sleep where.

Care of the Birds and Maintenance of Their Quarters

Softbills kept under proper conditions require no special care. They groom themselves, happily

A pair of Pekin robins sunbathing. The birds turn their raised feathers toward the sun, so that its rays can penetrate to the skin.

take daily baths, and wear their claws down through natural use. If the claws get too long (see drawing on page 14) or if the bill gets overgrown, there is something wrong about the way the birds are kept (see page 58).

Acclimation and Care

Bird showers

In an outdoor aviary you can let your birds take short showers by running water through a garden sprinkler or a perforated hose attached to the ceiling. Indoors you can water the plants in the room with a spray bottle while the birds are flying freely. Many softbills then eagerly use the wet plants to get themselves wet. Tame birds often like to be sprayed directly.

Caution: Never use a spray bottle that has been used with insecticides! Insecticides are deadly for birds. Whether the showers are administered indoors or out, never use warm water. Warm water dissolves the oils on the feathers so they no longer regulate the bird's body temperature properly.

Sunbathing

When softbills sunbathe, which they love to do, they raise their feathers to let the sun's rays penetrate to the skin (see drawing).

In an outdoor aviary you must be sure that there are shady as well as sunny areas to avert possible sunstroke.

If your birds live indoors you can take the cage to a balcony or garden to let them enjoy the sun. If the move is too upsetting for them, don't bother. If you do move them, check the spot to make sure it is not in the full sun without any shade at all.

Note: Remember that the shade is not constant but moves along with the sun.

Routine Maintenance

Daily: Change food (food that spoils easily should be changed twice a day in the hot weather); give fresh water after washing the dishes with warm water; remove leftover food; check appearance of droppings; observe the birds for their state of health; take care of live insects you're growing; change litter if necessary (do this routinely every 2 or 3 days); replace earth or pieces of sod in special container.

Weekly: Thoroughly clean cage or indoor aviary; wash food dishes and bathing vessels with dishwashing liquid (rinse thoroughly afterward); scrub perches and branches as necessary.

In an outdoor aviary the earth needs to be hoed, flagstones cleaned, and the entire structure checked carefully for holes in the wiremesh, mouse holes, and other problems. Examine the birds for signs of parasites (see Parasites, page 60). Tend the plants in the aviary.

Monthly: In cages and indoor aviaries with birds that eat fruit and nectar, replace sticky branches.

In outdoor aviaries, clean the ground thoroughly.

Twice a year: Collect droppings from birds in an outdoor aviary and have them analyzed.

Once a year: Paint the supporting structure of an outdoor aviary, and make any needed repairs.

Specific Questions Dealing with the Care of Softbills

Should the Birds Be Covered at Night?

In contrast to canaries and parakeets, softbills are made nervous rather than comforted if the cage is covered with a cloth. It is better to choose a location where the birds have peace and quiet at night than to use a cage cover.

Softbills in Winter

For birds that live indoors, wintering over is no problem. Our normal room temperatures agree with them.

Many softbills that spend summers in an outdoor aviary can be moved to a cool cellar during the winter. In dry weather they can even spend some time outdoors. Cold air does them no harm because, like our native birds, they can protect themselves against it by puffing up their plumage. Softbills that are wintered over like this are especially hardy and strong. If the weather stays cold and wet for any length of time, however, they can catch cold. Under these circumstances, softbills should be moved back indoors or stay in their shelter.

Wintering Birds in an Outdoor Aviary:

• The birds must be well acclimated and have spent the entire summer in the outdoor aviary.

• The aviary must be protected from the wind and part of it from precipitation.

• The birds must always have access to a warm shelter (59–64°F; 15–18°C).

• Food and water should be offered in the shelter; if the drinking water freezes, the birds can die of thirst.

• Always lock the birds into the shelter at night.

• At daytime temperatures below 20°F (–5°C), let the birds out for only an hour or so at a time.

• If birds living in an outdoor aviary are to be wintered over warm, bring them inside in September when the difference between indoor and outdoor temperatures is not yet too great. Caution: If the weather is already quite cold and it's considerably warmer inside, the birds may start their reproductive cycle too early. Return the softbills to the outdoors around the end of May when the danger of frost is past.

What Should You Do If Your Softbill Escapes?

If your softbill escapes and finds its way outdoors, this does not necessarily mean that the bird is gone forever.

Search: Most softbills naturally inhabit trees and bushes. Unlike other birds, such as most parrots, which are used to open space (steppes, deserts, and heaths), these softbills do not take off in panicked flight but are more likely to hide in the nearest bush. Your escaped bird is therefore probably waiting in a bush or tree nearby, and this is where you should begin your search.

Calling the bird: If the lost bird belongs to a social species and has been living with a partner, this partner can help you now. Put the cage with the

A hand-reared white-eye enjoys having its throat gently scratched.

remaining bird in the open window or on the balcony, and the lost one, if it hears its companion's calls, will respond promptly.

If a bird that is kept singly has flown off and you also have a pair of a social species, it's worth your while to see if their calls will bring the escapee back. Separate the two mates so that they cannot see each other but can hear each other's voices. There is a good chance that the familiar calls will lure back the lost one.

Note: As a precautionary measure you can make a tape of your bird singing to be used if the bird ever escapes.

The cage with a treat in it: Once you have located the escaped bird, set up its cage with a favorite treat in it where the bird can see it. It is a good idea to devise a way of shutting the cage door from a distance by means of a long thread, for instance, so that the bird doesn't take off again when you approach.

An outdoor aviary: Birds from an outdoor aviary usually find their way back more easily because they are used to the looks of their wider surroundings and the aviary is easy to recognize.

Pekin robins and a relative.
Above and below, left: Pekin robin (*Leiothrix lutea*).
Below, right: Blue-winged siva (*Siva cyanouroptera*).

Overleaf: Silver-eared mesias.
Above: Silver-eared mesia (*Leiothrix argentauris*). Below: A pair of red silver-eared mesias (*L. a. laurinus*) with the female in front and the male behind.

Dangers Inside and Outside

Source of Danger	Effects	How to Avoid
Bathroom	Escape through open window; sliding into toilet, sink, or filled bathtub and drowning; poisoning from cleansers and chemicals	Keep bird away from bathroom; never leave bathroom door open
Wire grating (in cage or aviary)	Escape through mesh that is too wide or has holes; sticking head through and strangling or getting stuck (serious injuries); injuries from rusted wire; cuts on toes and head from wire that is too thin	Select mesh appropriate to the size of your birds; check mesh regularly for rusting and holes; welded wire is best
Electric wires and outlets	Electrocution if birds peck in search of food (especially starlings and species feeding on nectar)	Hide wires inside the walls and disconnect exposed wires; pull plugs if you leave bird alone in room; cover outlets with safety plugs
Threads, string, tinsel, rubber bands, etc.	Strangling in loops; problems from ingesting foreign objects; poisoning	Don't leave these things lying around; keep bird away from Christmas tree.
Curtains	Birds can get caught in loose weave and break toes or legs in trying to get free; poisoning from nibbling on lead weights	Use curtains made of tightly woven material and without lead weights
Containers with water (vases, buckets, aquariums, bowls with water turtles)	Slipping in and drowning; in case of bowls with water turtles, danger of disease such as salmonellosis	Cover all bowls and containers; don't let bird fly freely during house cleaning
Knitted and crocheted items	Getting caught and strangling	Don't leave your knitting out; put away lacy doilies, etc.
Poisons	Poisoning: lead, verdigris, nicotine, rust, mercury, vapors from coated pans, all cleansers and pesticides, and contaminated food, insects are deadly; also harmful are pencil leads, tips of ballpoint and felt pens, alcohol, coffee, and hot spices	Remove all potentially harmful items and substances from the bird's living space and store them where the bird can't get at them
Windows and glass doors	Collision, possibly resulting in a concussion, fractured skull, or broken neck	Furnish all glass (windows, doors to balcony, glass walls) with curtains
Other pets (dogs, cats)	They make bird nervous, can bite or kill it	Never leave bird alone in same room with other pets, even in a cage (see page 7)
Kitchen stove	Burns, possibly fatal, from landing on hot burner	Don't let bird fly in kitchen unattended; put a covered pot of water on any unused hot burner

Dangers Inside and Outside

Source of Danger	Effects	How to Avoid
Candlelight	Burns, possibly fatal	Do without candlelight while your bird flies freely
Glues	Poisoning, often deadly, from evaporating solvents; getting glue on feathers, beak, or feet	Keep bird out of the room while you use glue (for repairs or crafts), and air room thoroughly before letting bird back in
Kitchen	A bird can choke to death from steam or vapors; the kitchen heat and subsequent airing can cause colds and other illness; bird may escape when windows are opened for airing	Don't keep a bird in the kitchen
Human beings	Getting stepped on (birds that like to be close to the ground); being sat on (very tame birds)	Be especially watchful when your bird is flying freely in the room
Plants	Poisoning, often fatal, from plants containing toxic substances (see page 32 for plants to be avoided in the aviary.) Cacti can cause extremely serious wounds if a bird lands on one.	Forego poisonous plants in the bird's room; *Cissus antarctica, Rhocissus,* hibiscus, and spiderworts are nonpoisonous
Cupboards and drawers	Starving to death or suffocating if the bird is locked in and its plight goes unnoticed	Always check carefully before shutting a drawer to make sure no bird is hiding in it
Pots and dishes	Drowning in liquid contents; scalding if liquid is hot (food and foamy liquids are mistakenly used for landing)	Cover pots and keep bird out of kitchen; don't let bird fly around during your meals
Chairs and couches	Getting squashed when people sit down (especially tame birds); possibly fatal injuries if you run over a bird with a chair on rollers	Before you sit down make sure there is no bird on the seat or on the floor
Sun	Sunstroke or heart attack if the sun is too strong	Bird cage can be in the sun, but bird must have a shady spot to retreat to
Cracks between furniture and walls	Sliding down, getting stuck; if the bird cannot free itself it may die of heart failure	Barricade cracks with wood or stiff cardboard
Pointed objects (ends of wire, nails, needles, splinters)	Injuries, deep puncture wounds	Don't leave such objects lying around; store them where bird can't get at them
Temperature fluctuations	Colds or freezing if temperature drops suddenly and drastically; heat stroke or heart attack in sudden great heat	Avoid abrupt changes in temperature; acclimate the bird slowly to new temperature
Drinking water	Dying of thirst if the dispenser is defective or empty or if the water has evaporated or is frozen; also if bird refuses to drink medicated water	Refresh water every day and always check dispenser; make sure the bird drinks if medication is added to water

Dangers Inside and Outside

Source of Danger	Effects	How to Avoid
Doors	Getting caught and squashed if door is shut quickly; escaping; sickness caused by drafts from open doors	Special vigilance
Pests	Internal and external parasites can cause disease	Perform all cleaning chores regularly and thoroughly; take appropriate measures if bird gets infested (see page 60)
Sinks and bathtubs	Slipping, drowning; birds may try to land on suds	Keep bird out of kitchen and bathroom
Detergents, cleansers chemicals	Poisoning if bird absorbs any of these	Keep all household cleansers in closed cupboards; carefully rinse off all traces after use
Vases, pitchers, glasses, etc.	Sliding in and getting stuck; suffocating, starving to death, or heart failure caused by fright	Fill empty vessels with bird sand or crumpled paper or cover them; store empty glasses upside down
Cigarettes, cigars	Smoke-filled air is harmful and nicotine is deadly; birds can get burnt on cigars or cigarettes resting on ashtrays	It's best not to smoke near birds; if someone does smoke, air regularly; never leave tobacco in any form in the same room–the bird might nibble on it.
Drafts	Colds, pneumonia	Avoid at all cost; check with a burning candle –the flame shows the slightest air current; supply plenty of wind protection in an outdoor aviary

Dangers Inside and Outside

Unsuitable or Poisonous Plants

The following plants are dangerous to softbills.

Caution: Don't gather any plants along the roadside or near cultivated fields that have been sprayed with pesticides.

Blue Laburnum (*Wisteria sinensis*)
Corn cockle
Datura
Dieffenbachia (all species)
Golden laburnum (*Laburnum anagyroides*)
Helleborus (all species)
Holly (*Ilex aquifolium*)
Hyacinth
Lantana
Lords and ladies (or cuckoo pint)
    (*Arum maculatum*)
Mistletoe

Monkshead, wolfsbane (and all other *Aconitum* species)
Narcissus
Nightshades (Solanaceae — all species)
Oleander
Periwinkle
Primrose
Privet (*Ligustrum vulgare*)
Rhododendron
Saxifrage
Snowdrop (*Galathus vulgare*)
Spurge
Spindle Tree (*Euronymus europaeus*)
Strychnus nux-vomica
Sweet pea
Thorn Apple (*Datura stamonium*)
Wax plant (*Hoya carnosa*)
Yew

Diet

Feeding softbills presents a much greater challenge for a bird owner than feeding most seed-eating birds. Many problems and illnesses softbills suffer from can be traced back to improper feeding and can be avoided if an appropriate, varied, and nutritious diet is supplied. The food you give your softbills should appeal to their taste, satisfy their appetite, and contain the necessary nutrients in the right combinations (see table on page 38).

Basic Food

Commercial Food for Insectivores

The basic food for softbills is a commercial mixture made up mostly of insects. It can be given to all softbills, including those that feed primarily on fruit and nectar, because it is rich in proteins and fiber. Pet stores sell several kinds of packaged food, each consisting of a somewhat different mixture appropriate to a different group of birds. Thus there are special mixtures for delicate feeders, for thrush-like birds, for starlings, and for mynahs. A so-called universal mixture is said by its manufacturers to suit all kinds of bills.

Commercial insect mixtures can be bought in ready-to-eat or in dry form.

Ready-to-Eat Mixture: This can be given to the birds as is; it is easy to store and keeps fresh for a while. There are two varieties: one with fat added and the other mixed with honey. The first is generally preferred by insectivores, the second by fruit-eating species.

Preparing your own honeyed mixture: Combine 8 ounces of dry packaged food with 1½ tablespoons heated honey and 1 teaspoon hot vegetable fat (unsalted and without spices!). Keep on the warm stove for about 15 minutes (for the honey and fat to be completely absorbed), and mix well. The mixture should have the consistency of loose flakes after cooling. Keeps for several days.

Dry Mixture: This food must be slightly moistened (by adding finely chopped fruit or carrot, for instance, or fruit juice or strained cottage cheese). In its dry state, commercial dry food keeps indefinitely, but once it's mixed it spoils very quickly (in hot weather it must be prepared fresh twice a day). The addition of items high in vitamins and minerals makes this an especially nutritious food.

Signs of quality: There should be a large proportion of recognizable elements, such as insects, tiny crustaceans, ant pupae, and dried berries, with very little floury stuff or crumbs. Check the mixture before you buy it, opening the package or asking to see a sample. A good-quality packaged food for softbills has a pleasant, aromatic smell and the consistency of loose flakes. A musty or rancid smell, clumps that don't disintegrate when lightly pressed, and webby filaments are signs of spoilage or of contamination with pests. Ask for another package if this is the case.

Nectar Drink

You can buy nectar drink as a dry powder that you then dissolve in warm water. This complete food for humming birds and other nectar feeders is also readily accepted by white-eyes and leafbirds. Commercially available nectar drink has the same sugar content as natural nectar but is also enriched with amino acids (essential elements of proteins), vitamins, minerals, and trace elements, all tailored to the needs of the birds.

Mixing your own: (Recipe courtesy of Karl-Ludwig Schuchmann, hummingbird expert, 1984): ½ ounce (15 g) fructose (half fruit sugar and half grape sugar), ⅙ ounce (5 g) of a protein supplement with added vitamins and minerals, 3 fluid ounces (90 ml) lukewarm water. This amount is enough for two nectarivorous birds for 1 day. Dissolve the fructose and the supplement in the water and stir with a wooden or plastic spoon (don't use an egg beater or electric mixer!). A metal spoon or excessive aeration can destroy a significant amount of the vitamins.

Note: The sugar content should never exceed 20 percent; too high a proportion of sugar can cause severe intestinal problems. Be sure to measure all quantities very carefully!

Additional Foods

The foods that are discussed in this section are meant to complement and enrich the birds' basic diet, but they should never be substituted for the basic food mixture.

Communal eating. Many social species, such as the white-eyes, don't mind company even at the food dish.

Fruits and Greens

Fruit is a natural part of a softbill's diet. It is rich in vitamins, fruit acids, minerals, and fiber. Fruit also has a high water content, however, and birds eating a lot of fruit produce mushy or wet droppings so that the litter or floor covering must be changed more frequently.

You can feed your softbills a wide variety of fruits and vegetables. Here are just a few examples:
• Wild and cultivated fruits, such as apples, pears, cherries, oranges, tangerines, bananas, grapes, raisins, kiwi fruit, figs, raspberries, strawberries, rowanberries, elderberries, firethorn (pyracantha) berries, and rosehips.

• Vegetables, like tomatoes and cucumbers (peeled).
• Greens, like chickweed, lettuce, parsley, spinach, and cress.

Note: Feed small amounts of fruits that are high in carbohydrates, like bananas, grapes, raisins, or figs, so that your softbill doesn't get fat. Also remember to use only unsprayed fruit and vegetables for your birds.

Tips for storing: Many fruits keep well frozen but they have to be completely thawed before they can be given to the birds. Berries can also be dried. Cress can be sowed in a pot on a windowsill and thus provide fresh greens in the middle of the winter.

Preparation: Depending on its size, fruit can be given whole or cut in half or diced. If you dice the fruit, make the pieces beak-sized; otherwise the birds knock the food against the perches or drop it on the floor where it can be contaminated.

Chop leafy greens finely, and mix in with the basic food.

Eggs

Eggs are an ideal food that almost all birds like. When fresh, eggs contain almost all the nutrients a bird needs.

Preparation: Boil the egg for 12 minutes, mash with a fork until fine, and mix with zwieback crumbs. Other things you can mix with the egg are baby cereal, powdered milk, wheat flakes, and vitamin and mineral supplements.

Note: Never give a bird raw or even partially cooked eggs. (There is serious danger of salmonella infection.) Always feed eggs in small amounts because they are so rich in protein and carbohydrates.

Honey

Honey has a high sugar content (approximately 75 percent) and is an ingredient in many nectar recipes. It is also used in the preparation of commercial food mixtures. Many nectarivorous softbills like honey thinned with water, but this is no

Diet

substitute for nectar drink because it lacks important nutrients.

Pollen

Pollen is a valuable food for softbills because of its high content of essential amino acids, minerals, trace elements, vitamins, fatty acids, and enzymes.

Preparation: You can buy pollen in pulverized form in natural food stores and some drugstores. Mix the powder with the basic food, egg food (see page 34), or nectar drink (see page 33).

Milk and Milk Products

These should be given to softbills only very sparingly because the birds cannot digest the sugar contained in milk (lactose) and may get sick from it.

Cottage cheese and other unfermented cheeses present no problem because they contain only negligible amounts of lactose. Cottage cheese, in fact, is highly recommended because of its valuable proteins and high mineral content.

Preparation: Use cottage cheese for moistening dry insect food, or add it, finely mashed, to the nectar drink.

Other Grocery Items

Fruit juices for babies, soy flour, wheat flakes, chopped nuts, and similar products high in nutrients can occasionally be given in addition to the basic food.

Meat and fish are good sources of protein; cooked beef heart and freshwater fish are especially recommended, but by no means all softbills accept them.

Other Supplemental Foods

The foods in the following list are designed to satisfy the nutritional needs of specific domestic or pet animals. An exclusive diet of any one of them would soon result in an excess of some nutrients for your softbill and a deficiency in others. As an addition to the basic diet, however, mixed in with it or with the egg food, they lend welcome variety.

Mynah pellets: These are sold in pet stores. You can feed these pellets to softbills but only in addition to a diet that is nutritious and varied and includes plenty of fruit. The larger softbills (Pekin robins and bulbuls) can eat them whole; for smaller ones the pellets must be broken or moistened.

Chick pellets: Commercial feed for poultry is very nutritious and popular with some softbills.

Various feed meals: Mash for laying hens and highly nutritious. Meat meal, fish meal, and blood meal are all high in protein, but in the long run they provide too limited a diet.

Dry dog food: Dog food usually contains cereals, egg, and meat. Bulbuls and Pekin robins often eat it without special preparation if water is added the night before to soften it.

Seeds: Many softbills eat semiripe or sprouted seeds. Pekin robins sometimes also accept regular birdseed, such as millet, canary, and crushed hemp seeds.

Live Food

Most softbills, including the frugivorous and nectarivorous kinds, eat small organisms like insects, spiders, millepedes, and worms, which supply them with protein. They also raise their young almost entirely on small prey, hardly resorting to soft foods at all. Thus, live food is a necessity for raising baby birds, and it also forms an important part of the adult birds' regular diet.

Sources of Live Food

Live insects like mealworms, maggots, crickets, and enchytraeids are sold by some pet stores year-round. You can also catch or raise your own live foods, however (see Growing Live Food, page 39).

Catching prey: There are a number of methods people used to employ to gather insects, like netting them in fields or over water, setting up light traps, or shaking tree branches with sheets or an open umbrella underneath to collect the catch. None of these should be used nowadays for a number of reasons:

• Some insect species are protected because they are endangered. You cannot legally collect these.

• Insects bred in nature may contain high levels of pesticides or may have absorbed other harmful substances from the environment; if used as food they may pose a threat to your softbills' health.

• Many worms and snails are carriers of parasites, which can be passed on to the birds.

Recommended methods: The methods that are described here are, of course, suitable only if the insects have had as little contact with pesticides as possible.

• Find branches with aphid-infested leaves and put them in the cage or aviary.

• The leaf mold of the forest floor contains more tiny organisms than you might believe. Put some of this soil in a flat container in the cage or aviary, and the birds will soon start pecking away at it.

• Grow some plants in an outdoor aviary that attract insects (such as evening primrose, elderberry, and native herbs).

A shama cock at the food dish. His head tilted, he is peering at the morsels with one eye only.

• Learn all you can about biologic methods of containing garden pests. If you garden according to organic principles, you may find you have a ready source of unpoisoned insects for your birds.

Breeding insects: There are no ecological or toxicological arguments against breeding insects as live food for birds. It's also possible to always have an adequate supply of them on hand. Because of these great advantages, an entire chapter is devoted to this topic (see Growing Live Food, page 39).

Feeding the Birds Right

Food and Feeding Stations

• The food must be in perfect condition and the food dishes in places that are out of the way of droppings, bathwater, and rain. Cleanliness is equally important in the case of drinking and bathwater.

• If you have a group of birds, make sure there are enough feeding stations and dishes so that the weaker birds get a chance to eat, too, and there are no fights over food.

• Offer the food in places that conform to the birds' natural feeding habits; in other words, put the food dishes for ground-dwelling birds on the floor and those for tree dwellers higher up.

• The morsels should fit the size of the beak and the food composition agree with the needs and tastes of the species it is intended for. For instance, mynah food should be in big chunks and made up largely of fruit; shamas like smaller bites and lots of insects, whereas white-eyes live mostly on fruit and nectar drink.

• If possible, supply food that keeps the birds busy for a while finding and eating it. Leave berries on the stems rather than picking them off and putting them in a dish; fresh branches with green leaves often have tiny bugs on them, and leaf mold from the woods is full of small animal life.

• Throw leftover food in the garbage rather than giving it to wild birds; it is probably spoiled or may contain pathogens. If the birds consistently leave

Basic Elements of a Good Diet

Element	Function	Occurs in	Special remarks
Protein	Primary building material for the organism	Natural prey (insects, worms, spiders); soft food, pellets, milk products, eggs	Greater need for protein during growth, molt, and reproductive period; amino acids (which the organism can't synthesize) are especially important
Carbohydrates	Energy source	Fruit, nectar, honey	Birds increase their intake of carbohydrates (berries, fruit) in the fall to acquire a layer of fat for winter
Fats	Stored energy for lean times	Animal prey; many fruits; prepared food with fat in it; nuts	Birds in captivity have reduced energy requirements; if food is too rich, birds tend to get fat
Vitamins	Diverse functions in metabolism; cannot be synthesized by organism and must be supplied in food	Present in food in various combinations; add vitamin supplements to drinking water or food	Increased need for vitamins during reproductive period and molt; before onset of either, give larger doses for a week; during and after illness, too, more vitamins are required
Minerals and trace elements	Many diverse functions in tissue formation and metabolism	Fruit, milk products; soil (fresh, not fertilized!); mineral supplements	Birds should always have a bowl with fresh soil; many food insects (e.g., larvae) are low in minerals and should be sprinkled with a supplement before being fed to birds
Water	Maintenance of body tissue; metabolic functions; dissolves and transports nutrients	Fresh tap water; uncarbonated mineral water	Plentiful supply of water is especially important for birds because of their high metabolic rate; their bodies store very little water (extra weight for flying!); a day and a half without water can be fatal; never give boiled water because boiling destroys minerals
Roughage	Stimulates intestinal activity; supplies no energy	Plants high in fiber; chitin and horny substances	Important for caged birds; lends a feeling of fullness without making fat

some food uneaten, check once more if you are giving them the right kinds and in the right amounts.

Amounts of Food

Traditional wisdom has it that a songbird must consume its own weight in food every day. This is only a rough estimate. The amount of food a softbill needs depends on
• what kind of food it eats
• the size of the cage or aviary (the more exercise the birds get, the more they can eat without danger of obesity)
• what stage of the yearly cycle they are in (during the courtship and mating period and during the molt birds need more protein; in the fall more fruit high in carbohydrates is appropriate)

• temperature (if birds are wintered over cool, they should get food high in carbohydrates; if they winter over indoors, they need food high in fiber but low in carbohydrates)

Feeding Times

Always feed the birds at the same set times because their whole daily routine revolves around their eating schedule. Supply fresh soft food in the morning. A fresh batch of soft food should be given in the afternoon, especially on hot summer days when food spoils easily (mixtures you prepare from scratch as well as nectar drink).

Birds are early risers. See to it that they have something to eat as soon as they start the day (packaged food or fruit).

Growing Live Food for Birds

Considerations Before Deciding to Grow Live Food

A number of insects that can be fed to softbills are easy to raise, and growing them yourself has many advantages. You are not diminishing potentially rare species as you may if you catch insects in the wild, and cultivated insects are always well nourished. Growing your own live food is generally cheaper than buying it, and if you plan things right, you'll always have enough live food on hand.

Many insects that might be fed to softbills are serious household pests, however, and great cau-

tion is always in order when growing insects to make sure they don't get loose and do damage. Voracious insects like cockroaches and larder beetles should be avoided for this reason.

Make sure that the food you feed the insects is free of pesticides. Wash greens carefully, and peel fruit to be on the safe side. Many chemicals added to foods to protect them against pests can prove harmful to your colony of cultivated insects. Also remember that many insects develop immunities to pesticides and that the poisons are then passed on to your birds.

Mealworms

The most common insect fed to birds is the mealworm, which isn't a real worm at all but the larva of the darkling beetle (*Tenebrio molitor*). Mealworms are easy to grow and to store.

Mealworms are readily eaten by all softbills, but they are not an ideal live food. If fed in too great quantities, mealworms can lead to health problems in birds, such as sores on the feet and eye problems.

Possible causes that have been suggested: The mealworms may interfere with the body's absorption of vitamins; they may be too fatty; or their chitinous shells may lack minerals or contain poisonous substances.

Solution: Sprinkle vitamin and mineral supplements on the mealworms before feeding them to the birds; give only moderate amounts (6 to 10 per day for a bird the size of a Pekin robin. It's best to give freshly hatched larvae and pupae (they don't yet have solid chitinous shells) or freshly hatched beetles, which are whitish and don't develop their tough, black shells until after a couple of days.

What You Should Know Before You Start: You can buy mealworms at pet stores year-round. Growing your own is cheaper than buying them only if you have a flock of birds or if you want to raise baby softbills, which requires large quantities of preferably small mealworms.

Food insects that are easy to grow.

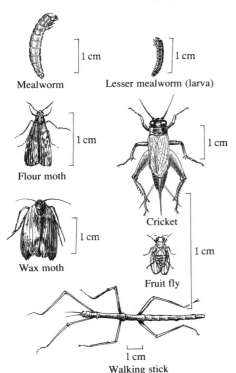

Mealworm — 1 cm

Lesser mealworm (larva) — 1 cm

Flour moth — 1 cm

Cricket — 1 cm

Wax moth — 1 cm

Fruit fly — 1 cm

Walking stick — 1 cm

Growing Live Food

If you have a number of softbills or plan to raise baby birds, you should make sure you have plenty of mealworms, buying half a pound or a whole pound as your basic stock. The advantage is that you can feed the mealworms optimally before storing them and that you will then always have a supply of freshly hatched larvae that are low in chitin.

Raising Mealworms

Container: Fill some smooth-walled, shallow plastic containers with wheat bran on which you place egg cartons, corrugated cardboard, old rags, or something similar for the mealworms to hide under. Cover the containers tightly with gauze or other cloth because the beetles can fly.

Food: The beetles and the larvae need bran, raw oatmeal, laying mash, soy meal, breadcrumbs, and fresh fruit and vegetables (e.g., apples, sprouted grains or soybeans, carrots, or turnips). The fresh food should be eaten by the insects every day so that the bran doesn't get wet. Otherwise mildew may develop.

Temperature and life cycle: The surrounding temperature and the availability of food affect how quickly the beetles develop. Under optimal conditions (80°F; 27°C) it takes 10 to 12 weeks for an egg to develop into an adult beetle. At temperatures around 68° F (20°C) the same process takes close to 6 months.

Stages of development: Eggs are dropped in the bran; minute larvae (mealworms) hatch and grow a number of new skins as they grow and before they turn into pupae, from which they emerge as beetles. You can delay the pupal stage by keeping the larvae in a cool place.

Lesser Mealworm

The lesser mealworm (*Alphitobius diaperinus*) becomes a shiny black beetle somewhat smaller than the darkling beetle and about the size of a ladybug. Like the mealworm, it is a pest and also makes an excellent live food for birds.

Feed this insect only in its larval stage, when it measures about ⅜ inch (1 cm) and is an ideal size for small softbills like white-eyes.

What You Should Know Before You Start: Pet stores sell lesser mealworms only rarely, but you can sometimes find breeding colonies advertised for sale in specialized magazines.

Lesser mealworms are often found where grain or animal feed is stored. Never use beetles that come from a poultry farm because they may carry and transmit pathogens.

Raising Lesser Mealworms

Containers and food: The requirements are the same as for mealworms (see page 40).

Temperature and life cycle: The beetles require 5 to 8 weeks to grow to maturity in temperatures of 77°F (25°C) or more; it's pointless to try to raise them at temperatures below 68°F (20°C) because they grow so slowly and reproduce poorly.

Crickets

Raising crickets makes sense because they are easy to grow and prolific. There are a number of suitable species, among them the house cricket (*Acheta domesticus*) and the spotted field cricket (*Gryllus bimaculatus*). Crickets can be given at any stage of development, whenever they are the right size for your particular birds.

Live crickets can be fed only to birds in solid glass cages. If your birds live in a wire cage or an aviary, the crickets must be killed before they can be fed to the birds. Here is a suggestion of how to go about it: When a batch of crickets has reached the desired size, stick the egg cartons under which the creatures are still resting into a freezer bag first thing in the morning, tie it shut, and stick it in the freezer (not the refrigerator!). This way the crickets are killed quickly and painlessly and their full nutritional value is preserved.

Note: Replace old, dirty egg cartons with new ones the night before you plan to kill the crickets; this will yield a nice, clean harvest.

What You Should Know Before You Start: You can buy crickets for breeding at pet stores. Remember that they escape easily because they have powerful jumping legs. Also, their loud chirping gets on many people's nerves.

Raising Crickets

Containers: You need two enclosed terrariums (16 × 10 inches; 40 × 25 cm) at least 12 inches (30 cm) high so that the crickets won't jump out when you take off the top. Use window screening for vents. Or you can get plastic terrariums with tops that have narrow slits in them for ventilation. Necessary equipment: egg cartons piled on top of each other for the crickets to hide in; an electric bulb (25 watt) that is turned on about 12 hours a days for heat; shallow dishes for food; a water dispenser (don't offer water in dishes because small crickets may drown in it); a pot 4 or 5 inches tall filled with fresh earth in which the crickets lay eggs. The earth should be kept damp but not wet. Instead of earth you can use the moss used by florists to arrange flowers. The bottom of the terrarium is covered with sand or cat litter and must always be dry so that the female does not lay her eggs there.

Food: Pet food or animal feed (dog food or rabbit pellets, for instance) ground and mixed with fresh vegetables and fruit of all kinds.

Temperature and life cycle: If kept at 77°F (25°C), the tiny baby crickets, barely the size of ants, hatch after about 2 weeks. At 68°F (20°C), the process takes about 3 weeks. (This applies to house crickets; field crickets need more warmth.) Crickets live for about 12 weeks.

Note: Take out the egg-laying pot after 12 to 14 days and replace it with a new one. Put the old pot in the second terrarium so that the baby crickets can

hatch undisturbed and are not eaten by the older crickets.

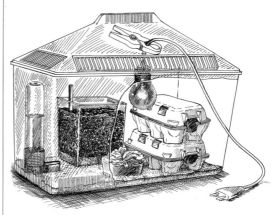

A breeding container for crickets. It must be quite tall, and the ventilation slits in the top must be narrow so that the crickets can't jump out through them.

Walking Sticks

Some species, such as the Indian walking stick (*Carausius morosus*), are easy to raise and prolific. They can be used as feed at any stage (anywhere from ½ to 2½ inches; 1–6 cm) to suit the needs of different birds. For softbills, specimens between ½ and 1½ inches (1–3 cm) are best. Walking sticks are an excellent food because, living entirely on vegetable matter, they are a good source of carotene (which is convertible to vitamin A).

When feeding walking sticks to birds, place them on flat, white dishes. Otherwise the birds have trouble seeing them because of their protective coloring and rigid immobility (walking sticks are nocturnal).

What You Should Know Before You Start: Walking sticks are generally not available at pet stores. Possible sources are zoological institutes or supplier's advertisements in magazines for terrarium enthusiasts.

Growing Live Food

Walking sticks, unlike crickets and grasshoppers, don't jump and are therefore easier to handle.

Almost all walking sticks are females; males are very rare, and reproduction occurs primarily through parthenogenesis.

Raising Walking Sticks

Container: Use a terrarium tightly covered with screening or gauze (be sure to provide adequate ventilation); place in it plants stuck into jars with narrow tops and filled with water. Cover the bottom with sand or absorbent paper towels.

Food: Fresh branches (as of deciduous trees, ivy, etc.); spiderworts; no additional water will be necessary.

Temperature and life cycle: At room temperature the eggs hatch after 13 to 20 weeks.

Drosophila Fruit Flies

There are a number of species of *Drosophila* flies (also known as vinegar flies) that measure only about 1 mm, including some strains that cannot fly. Fruit flies are readily eaten by birds and are a valuable source of protein, especially for smaller softbills like the white-eyes. They also add welcome variety to the diet of baby birds.

If your birds live in a glass cage, you can give them vinegar flies that can fly; otherwise you should stick to the flightless kind. You can simply put a portion of flies in the drawer at the bottom of the cage.

If your birds live in an outdoor aviary or a birdhouse, place a bucket of fruit peelings with some flies in the aviary. Cover the bucket with wire mesh (mesh approximately ½ inch; 1 cm) so that the birds cannot get at fermenting fruit and juices.

What You Should Know Before You Start: Breeding colonies of *Drosophila* flies are available at some pet stores. You may also find advertisements for them in magazines for aviculturists. In the summer, fruit flies gather on ripe fruit that is left out, where they can easily be caught.

Raising Fruit Flies

Container: Use old cans and jars with wood shavings or wire mesh in them, or anything else the flies can attach themselves to. Cover the jar tightly with gauze or a nylon stocking.

Food: Fruit flies feed on the microorganisms that develop in fermenting fruit juices and these organisms' products.

• Some fruits you can use are bananas and oranges. Be careful: Peel the fruit because residues from pesticides can be absorbed by the flies and passed on to the birds. Also, fermenting fruit starts to smell bad.

• Another possibility is to chop and mash fruit and add vinegar, yeast, vitamins, sugar, and bran or dry oatmeal.

• There are also commercial mixes in powder form to which water is added. These smell much less.

Temperature and life cycle: Room temperature is adequate (not below 68°F; 20°C). In a span of 2 weeks a female lays about 300 eggs from which the flies hatch in another 2 weeks.

Flour Moths

Flour moths (*Ephestia kuehniella* and related species) are household pests that are easy to raise. Birds like to eat them both as small moths (wing span ¾ inch; 2 cm) and as larvae.

The larvae can be picked out of the breeding container with tweezers. If you put the container in the refrigerator for awhile, the moths stop moving almost entirely so that they, too, can easily be transferred with tweezers.

What You Should Know Before You Start: You cannot buy flour moths. You may find them in cereal products or birdseed or even in the box where you raise mealworms. You can spot them by the webby clumps inside which the caterpillars live. Be careful. Don't try to breed them indoors! Raise them only in a birdhouse, and not even there if colonies of other insects that feed on flour or meal (lesser mealworms or mealworms) are housed there. Some moths inevitably escape and are bound to establish themselves in the container with the other insects.

Breeding Flour Moths

Container: Use a container tightly covered with wire screening to allow for ventilation. Choose the finest screening you can find. Don't use screening made of cloth or plastic because the caterpillars chew their way through both materials. Have the container half full with food litter on which you place a few layers of corrugated cardboard for the creatures to hide under and pupate.

Food: Bran, chick feed, laying mash, or similar kinds of food.

Temperature: Room temperature.

Wax Moths

The greater (*Galleria mellonella*) and the lesser (*Achroea grisella*) wax moths — two other leptidopterous insects — are parasites that live in beehives, where they cause significant damage by eating the honeycombs and spinning webs around the bee larvae. Wax moths, like flour moths, can be fed to birds either at the larval stage or as moths.

What You Should Know Before You Start: You can get wax moths from beekeepers. They are harder to raise than flour moths, but there is less risk of their escaping because wax moths thrive only where there is plenty of wax and warmth.

Raising Wax Moths

Container: House the wax moths just like flour moths; their caterpillars, too, like to pupate hidden in corrugated cardboard.

Food: Fill the container half full with old honeycombs, which you should be able to obtain from beekeepers.

Temperature and life cycle: Wax moths must be kept dark and quite warm. At the optimal temperature of 80 to 82°F (27–28° C), they mature in 6 to 7 weeks.

Enchytraeids

Enchytraeus albidus is a worm belonging to the family Enchytraeidae, sometimes referred to as potworms. *E. albidus* is a threadlike, white worm up to 2 inches (5 cm) long and is readily eaten by softbills.

The potworms gather around the food in their containers and can then be picked up with a fork. Feed them to the birds in a flat dish without removing the small clumps of earth that stick to them. The earth is a good source of minerals for the birds.

What You Should Know Before You Start: Breeding colonies of enchytraeids are often available at pet stores.

Growing enchytraeids is easy, but the worms are quite delicate. The soil must be kept moist (not wet) and loose at all times. If conditions are not quite perfect, mites and molds can invade the soil. Before embarking on worm raising, you should do some calculations to see if the venture is worth your while or whether you are better off buying the worms at the pet store.

Raising Enchytraeids

Container: Fill a flat wooden box with loose soil high in organic matter (a mixture of unfertilized potting soil, leaf mold, and peat moss).

Food: Combine some oatmeal, grated carrots, baby cereal, a vitamin supplement, and milk, and bring to a quick boil. The mixture should be thick enough to stick together. Spread a thin layer over one area of the box, and cover lightly with some earth (to discourage mold). Don't give more than what is eaten within 2 days.

Temperature and life cycle: If the worms are kept dark and at room temperature, they develop to maturity in about 3 weeks.

Insects You Should Not Raise Yourself

Maggots

Maggots are the larvae of a species of blowfly or bluebottle fly and are about ⅜ inches (1 cm) long. They can be bought at pet stores and sometimes at fishing tackle shops.

Storage: Keep the maggots cool in containers with bran. If they are kept warm, they pupate within a few days. Many adult birds accept the maggots for feeding to their young.

Note: Make certain that the maggots cannot escape from the container.

Bee Larvae

Use the drone larvae of honeybees. They can be obtained from beekeepers.

Storage: Freeze the larvae in their honeycombs, and break larvae to be fed to birds out of the combs while still frozen. Bee larvae are good for raising baby birds, especially if the birds must be hand reared (see page 52).

Ant Pupae

You can buy these either dried or frozen at pet stores, and they are an excellent addition to soft or raising food.

Note: Sprinkle some mineral supplement over maggots, bee larvae, and ant pupae before feeding them to the birds.

Aphids

Aphids are found on infested plants. Leave them on the plants, and put shoots and branches into the cage or aviary.

The rufous-bellied niltava (*Niltava sundara*) is not only a spectacularly colored representative of the Muscicapidae family but also has a lovely voice.

Raising Softbills

Success in raising baby birds is the ultimate achievement for a bird fancier specializing in softbills and proves beyond any doubt that the birds are properly kept and happy.

To Breed or Not to Breed

If you want to breed your birds, you should first plan what you are going to do with the young birds if there are any. For in most cases the parents will want to get rid of them as soon as they are fully grown, if not before, and will start chasing them as rivals. At this point the young birds need cages or aviaries of their own, and if you have no space for them you should join a bird club (see Addresses, page 96) as early as possible. Through a club you can get in contact with other fanciers of similar interests who may not only provide good homes for birds you are unable to keep but who may also be interested in swapping birds. This gives you an opportunity to combine new pairs and avoid the danger of inbreeding. You can also approach pet dealers; many will be happy to take excess birds off your hands.

If you don't want to breed your birds, here are some tips on how to keep the birds happy without producing unwanted offspring.

• Social birds should always be kept at least in a twosome, but don't give them any opportunity to build a nest (no nest boxes or nesting materials).

• If your softbills manage to construct a nest all the same, let them proceed, but replace their eggs with artificial ones. If you simply remove the eggs, the female would immediately lay more; this way she

A *pair of red-eared bulbuls during courtship ritual.* The female, on the right, is inviting the male to mate.

will sit on the nest until her broodiness passes, which takes longer than the normal incubation time.

• Even single females, or two that are "mated," sometimes build nests. Again, don't try to stop them, or they may keep laying eggs until physically exhausted. If there is no male of the same or a closely related species present, you don't need to exchange eggs since they are infertile.

Necessary Conditions for Breeding Birds

Selecting a Breeding Pair

A common problem bird fanciers wanting to breed their birds encounter is that there are no obvious external differences between the two sexes. Since the primary sexual organs are within the abdominal cavity, one must rely on differences in plumage, shape or size, voice, and behavior to sex the birds. There are some softbills with clearly distinguishable sexual characteristics, however, for

Members of the Muscicapidae family.
Above: A male dayal (*Copsychus saularis*). Below, left: a pair of shamas (*C. malabaricus*) with the male on the right and the female on the left. Below, right: A pair of dama thrushes (*Geokichla citrina*) with the male on the left and the female on the right.

instance the shama, the dayal, the dama thrush, the Pekin robin, the orange-bellied leafbird, and the rufous-bellied niltava. With gold-fronted leafbirds, snowy-headed robin chat, mynahs, white-eyes, and bulbuls, it is difficult to tell the sexes apart.

The best way to end up with a mating pair is to watch a flock over an extended period until pairs form, or you can sometimes swap birds with other breeders.

Even when you have located a proper pair, there may still be trouble ahead. With solitary birds like shamas or feisty ones like the leafbirds, the partners have to be introduced to each other slowly and carefully (see pages 71 and 81).

Housing

It is possible to raise softbills in a cage, an indoor aviary, or a bird room, but an outdoor aviary is far preferable. The location should be as free from disturbances (from people, pets, other birds, and weather) as possible and the space set up to accommodate the courtship behavior of the particular species.

Birds whose courtship involves wild chases should have lots of open space, whereas more aggressive softbills, like shamas and leafbirds, need opportunities for the female to hide (plantings or loosely piled twigs).

Preparations for Nest Building

In nature, birds find their own nesting sites and nesting materials, but in captivity they need some help from their caretakers.

Enclosed nest boxes with removable tops that allow you to check occasionally on the nest.

• Collect a supply of nesting materials, such as coconut fibers (available at pet stores), stalks of grass, fine roots, moss, and animal hair ahead of time, and be sure to put them in the cage or aviary when you notice the very first signs of courtship behavior.

• It is easier for the softbills to build their nests in a good place if you provide them with the right kind of vegetation or artificial nest supports.

Left: A half-open nest box. Right: A nest basket. This kind of nest base is usually accepted by Pekin robins, white-eyes, and bulbuls.

• You can also encourage nest building by supplying nest boxes or nesting baskets (see drawings). Don't give them old birds' nests you may have found in the garden or the woods. These are unhygienic.

• Provide extra shelter against rain (from above and the sides) if the pair has chosen a spot in the outdoor aviary that has no roof over it.

Note: Sometimes softbills reject a nest box or basket until it is placed in a spot where they themselves have made an attempt to build a nest.

Planning the Food Supply

Start early enough to raise or buy live food (mealworms, lesser mealworms, crickets, wax moths, maggots, or bee larvae), for softbills raise their young almost exclusively on insects. Don't rely primarily on one kind of live food because parent birds sometimes refuse a certain kind of insect from one day to the next even though they have been feeding it to their young happily up to that point.

Raising Softbills

Note: Start increasing the proportion of live food in the parents' diet before the mating season begins, giving them all kinds of insects. This way you find out what they like, and the extra protein strengthens their reproductive drive. Keep on feeding them their regular soft food, too, so they will not lose their taste for it.

Mating and Incubation

The mating process is a complicated business, in which many factors play a role, such as the time of year, the physical environment, hormonal processes, food, and behavior patterns. A hitch in just one of these areas can be enough to thwart the whole enterprise.

Mating Season

Depending on their area of distribution, softbills living in the wild may mate in the summer or winter or during rainy seasons. In captivity, particularly if they are kept in an outdoor aviary, they adjust to our local seasons and usually reproduce in the spring or summer.

Courtship and Pair Formation

Courtship precedes the formation of pairs and is more or less violent, depending on the species.

Pairs of softbills living in the wild usually stay together for only one mating cycle, but in captivity pairing is often permanent. Even in species that are very gregarious and ordinarily live in flocks, partners live in exclusive pairs during the reproductive period. It is very important to take this into account when planning to let softbills breed.

Nest Location

Different species of softbills have very different requirements. Bulbuls are less fussy than other softbills; Pekin robins, leafbirds, and white-eyes

A brooding white-eye. The bottom of the nest consists of cotton wool, into which a small, cup-shaped nest made of coconut fibers has been woven.

prefer to nest on branches; shamas like enclosed or semienclosed cavities, whereas starlings always breed in holes.

Egg Laying

After the courtship is over, the pairs have formed, and the nests are built, the females start laying eggs at the rate of one per day. The egg of a typical songbird weighs almost a third of the female's body weight. If you consider that an average clutch consists of 3 to 4 eggs, you can appreciate what a feat this represents and what a drain it is on the female. You will understand how important optimal nutrition is and that for the sake of her health, a female should not be allowed to go through the process more than at most three times a year (remove nest boxes and nesting materials).

Incubation

Incubation may begin as soon as the first egg is laid or not until the laying of the last or second to last egg. Depending on when the female starts sitting on the eggs, the young hatch either all at once or one at a time. In the latter case the chicks may vary quite a bit in size as they grow up.

In some softbills, the male takes turns sitting on the eggs and in others the female does all the incubating, with the male helping only later when the nestlings must be fed. In some cases the male may interfere with incubation or even destroy the eggs. If that happens, he will have to be taken out of the cage the next time as soon as the first egg has been laid and be kept separately during the incubation period. Ordinarily the entire clutch is fertilized by one mating.

Length of Incubation

The eggs of most songbirds hatch after about 12 to 14 days. Some white-eyes have an exceptionally short incubation period that lasts only 10 days and a few hours, a record not only among softbills but among birds in general.

Development of the Young

There is no such thing as a prematurely born bird because a chick cannot break out of its shell until it is strong enough to peck its way out. This task is accomplished with the help of an "egg tooth" (a small projection on the bill). There are two ways to tell that the eggs have actually hatched:
• The parents usually carry the empty shells out of the box and deposit them in an out-of-the-way spot of the aviary.
• The behavior of the parent birds changes. Before the eggs have hatched, the parents always settle down on the nest quickly. After the hatching, they are more excited, perch on the edge of the nest longer, peer into the nest cavity, and they may have food in the beak. Naturally, as the hatchlings grow larger and larger, their need for food increases and their demands become more and more insistent.

Developmental stages of a white-eye nestling:

Day 2 after hatching: The body is still completely naked, and the eyes are closed.

Day 5: The feathers on the wings, back, and flanks are ready to burst out of their sheaths the next day, and the eyelids are getting ready to open.

Day 10: The bird is now entirely covered with feathers except around the eyes and the throat. The fleshy edge around the gape is still quite visible. The eyes have been open for about 2 days.

The Nestling Period

A chick stays in the nest about as long as it takes the eggs to incubate, sometimes several days longer. Baby birds reared in captivity often take even longer to leave the nest, particularly if there have been any problems.

Baby birds are born naked, blind, and completely helpless. During their first few days out of the shell, they are kept warm almost constantly by the parents, but as their feathers grow in, they are left alone in the nest more and more. The plumage now protects them enough against the cold, and the parents are kept busy foraging for food.

Rearing

Other softbills should be kept out of the rearing cage or aviary while young birds are being raised. They would only compete for the rearing food, which is usually not overly plentiful so that not enough would be left for the parent birds. It is best to divide the day's ration of live food into several portions to be given over the course of the day. After 3 or 4 weeks the fledglings are usually capable of fending for themselves and no longer depend on their parents for food.

Raising Birds Where the Parents Can Fly Freely

If you have a garden an outdoor aviary and some courage, you should try this method. Open a little door in the aviary grating through which the parent birds can come and go as they please (but not until the chicks have hatched), so that they can catch insects in the garden. As long as the young are in the nest, the parents will return to them faithfully. Be sure to close off the opening in time (about a day before the fledglings are ready to leave the nest), for if the entire family leaves the aviary, the birds are not likely to come back. Youngsters that are raised like this are noticeably better developed because they have a wider range of food available to them.

If you choose to raise birds under these conditions, keep in mind the following:
• The parent birds must be well acclimated and feel

White-eye nestlings being fed. The nestlings are almost ready to fledge. Their plumage is fully developed except for the eye ring.

at home in their surroundings, and they must be able to see the garden from their aviary so that they are in familiar territory the first time they venture out.
• The birds should not be shy, but neither should they be hand tame because you don't want them to fly up to strangers and possibly be caught. Tell your neighbors, in any case, that your birds may be flying loose.

• The opening in the aviary should not be too large (about the same size as a cage door), and it must be protected against cats.
• The opening should be visually obvious from the outside to make a hurried dash to safety possible (mount a perch in a good strategic location).
° Close the aviary in the evening (as soon as the birds have returned to it), and keep it locked overnight.
• This method is feasible only if the aviary is inhabited by the one bird family only.
• During the first few days, while one of the partners sits quietly on the nest warming the nestlings, other softbills of the same species housed in neighboring aviaries can be of help. With their calls they make it easier for the free-flying partner to find its way back.

Raising Softbills

• You cannot let more than one pair of the same species fly freely at the same time if they live near each other. The stronger pair would treat the weaker birds as rivals and chase them out of the garden.

• Even though free-flying parent birds do forage, you still have to give them plenty of insect food.

• If you have neighbors with cats, if you have seen a sparrow hawk circling overhead, or if pesticides are used heavily nearby, the risk of letting your softbills search for wild insects for their young is too great.

Hand-rearing Baby Birds

You have no choice but to try to hand-rear the chicks if their parents neglect them or stop feeding

Hand rearing a nestling. The baby bird is sitting in a man-made nest. It has accepted people as surrogate parents and is opening its gape in a begging display at the sight of a human hand

them altogether.

Housing: Remove the nestlings from the breeding cage or aviary along with the nest, or make them a new nest. A flower pot will do, and a layer of hay works well as padding because the toes can get a good grip, which provides healthy exercise for the feet.

Until the chicks develop their plumage you should cover them with a soft cloth and provide warmth with a lamp. The temperature should be between 86°and 100°F (30–38°C). If the chicks are cool and clammy to the touch, the temperature is too low; if they pant, it is too hot.

Food: Insects, such as bee larvae, are good for hand-feeding, but they have to be coated with a vitamin and mineral supplement. You can also prepare a substitute for live food made of strained cottage cheese and baby cereal, to which hard-boiled egg, ground beef, beef heart, packaged softbill food, or chick feed is added and which must be enriched with vitamins, essential amino acids, minerals, and a pinch of commercial hummingbird food.

Feeding: The food should be moistened until it sticks together so that you can pick it up easily with blunt tweezers or on a small, flat stick with rounded edges. Follow these suggestions when feeding the chicks:

• Give the chicks a few drops of water from your finger tips after every meal.

• Feed them small portions frequently. During the first half of the nestling period (5 or 6 days) they should be fed every quarter hour for about 14 hours a day, later every half hour for the same length of day.

• Before the chicks' eyes open, a few whistled notes or a gentle tap against the nest will make the nestlings open their beaks wide in anticipation of food.

• If the nestlings have already seen their parents, however, they are at first reluctant to accept food from humans, and for a while they need to be gently force fed.

• If you have to force feed a bird, hold its head carefully between thumb and index finger and use your other hand to squeeze the food into the oral cavity with the tweezers or flat wooden stick until the swallowing reflex is triggered.

• If the food composition is right, the nestlings' droppings are enveloped in a thin membrane and can easily be picked up with tweezers. If the droppings are messy and liquid, you should reconsider the diet. Hand-reared chicks often mature more slowly than parent-fed ones and often require feeding for 4 weeks or even longer.

Important note: Hand-reared birds are exceptionally tame. Still, you should not hand-rear chicks unless absolutely necessary because they do not grow up into fully normal adults. Softbills that have been reared by humans in isolation from other birds can become completely imprinted to humans (see drawing on page 26), which usually means that they cannot be used for breeding.

Leg Bands

You can obtain leg bands from a local bird club or write to the headquarters of national bird associations (see Addresses, page 96) for them. Leg bands are used by breeders for identification purposes and to record breeding information in code. Leg bands come in different sizes for different types of birds and can be slipped on the foot only until the bird is about 8 days old. If you use a second band of colored plastic, later you will find it easier to tell the birds apart. Leg bands are necessary if you plan to enter your birds in a bird show. They serve as proof of the birds' background.

Cross-breeding

The deliberate breeding of hybrids should be rejected as a matter of principle, for our breeding efforts should be aimed exclusively at preserving existing species and, where applicable, subspecies.

However, the question of whether to interfere with two birds that belong to different but closely related species, that have formed an attachment to each other in the absence of proper partners, and that obviously want to mate is one that every bird owner should settle in his or her own conscience. Bulbuls and white-eyes are particularly prone to cross-breeding.

Health Care and List of Diseases

Preventive Medicine

Many health problems and sicknesses softbills are subject to can be avoided if you pay close attention to preventive measures. Among these are:
• proper care and environmental conditions that suit the needs of the particular species
• strict cleanliness
• avoidance of situations that give rise to stress (too many birds living together, stronger birds molesting weaker ones, ongoing rivalries, interference from the surroundings)
• a balanced diet
• regular analysis of the droppings to keep tabs on the birds' state of health

Note: It is a good idea to ask another bird fancier to have a look at your birds now and then; a knowledgeble outsider is more likely to notice changes than the person who looks after them every day.

The Quarantine Cage

You will need a quarantine cage if you house several softbills together. Such a cage is useful
• for introducing new birds to their new home and for you to observe their state of health
• for isolating sick birds and protecting them from their fellows
• for preventing diseases from spreading to healthy birds

A quarantine cage is essentially a box cage that should be at least 20 inches (50 cm) wide. It is better if the front of the cage is made of grating rather than solid glass because the grating allows better ventilation and also prevents a build-up of heat when you use a heat lamp. It is also easier for a new bird to become familiar with its surroundings if it is behind bars rather than solid glass (see page 13). The floor should be lined with paper towels that are changed daily. This way it stays clean, and you can examine the droppings easily. In a quarantine cage plastic perches are preferable to natural branches because they can be cleaned and disinfected better.

Sick birds need more warmth than healthy ones. Place a heat lamp in front of the cage in such a way that it shines into only part of the cage (the temperature should not rise above 100° F; 38°C). The rest of the cage should stay around 68°F (20°C). A heat lamp gives off enough light for a bird to be able to eat and drink even at night. The lamp should be left on without interruption because short periods of exposure are ineffective. Any cage that has been used for a sick bird must afterward be cleaned and disinfected thoroughly.

Note: Put the food and water dishes at the cool end of the cage.

Disinfecting a Cage

A normal dishwashing detergent is generally adequate for washing a cage and the items in it (rinse well with clean water!). Exposure to the fresh air and sunlight also helps kill germs. Disinfectants should be used only in case of sickness. If you do use a disinfectant, make sure it is a mild one that contains no formaldehyde and that does not irritate the skin because birds are very sensitive to the slightest trace of formaldehyde even after thorough rinsing.

Note: Keep in mind that the same antiseptic is not effective against all pathogens and that several substances may be required to combat viruses, bacteria, fungi, and parasites.

Checking the Birds' Droppings

If you are keeping a number of birds, it is advisable to collect their droppings at regular intervals (preferably four times a year or at least in the spring and fall) and have the veterinarian analyze them for pathogens. This allows you to nip a disease in the bud. An analysis of fecal droppings is particularly important if the birds live in an outdoor aviary where pathogens can easily be transmitted to them in the droppings of wild birds or in prey (worms and snails).

Health Care and List of Diseases

When you collect the droppings, it is not necessary to get fecal matter from every bird; one sample per aviary is sufficient. In the morning, place a board covered with plastic or a sheet of thick plastic under the branches where the birds perch regularly. Pick up the droppings in the evening and keep them in a cool place until the next morning, when you take them to the vet. If the feces are to be examined for bacteria, speed is more critical. If the samples are not analyzed promptly, other, faster growing bacteria may crowd in on the pathenogenic ones so that the latter are hard to detect.

Worming birds makes sense only if a fecal analysis has revealed the presence of parasites. Each worming drug is aimed at one kind of worm and is ineffective against others; even broad-spectrum worming medicines do not kill all worms.

If a bird doesn't have worms, treatment with a worming medication is an unnecessary strain on the organism.

Autopsy

If some birds in a flock come down with an undiagnosed illness or die, or if you suspect an infectious disease, an autopsy of the dead birds is called for so that further losses can be prevented. The dead bird should be sent as fast as possible (express mail) to the nearest veterinary hospital or laboratory. Call ahead to arrange for a postmortem examination. If it is a weekend or the next day is a holiday, the dead bird should be kept refrigerated or possibly frozen.

A Medicine Cabinet for Birds

To provide first aid in an emergency and for routine procedures you always should have the following items on hand:
• scissors, nail clippers, pointed and blunt tweezers
• paper towels, absorbent cotton, cotton-tipped swabs
• iodine, ferric chloride
• an antibiotic eye ointment
• a drinking straw or something similar for splinting a leg
• adhesive tape and gauze bandages
• a medicine dropper or syringe
• disinfectant for washing hands and objects
• clean containers with screw-on lids to contain sample droppings

Signs of Illness

External signs are relatively obvious. They include bleeding, discharge from orifices, lumps, and broken bones.

With some sicknesses, the outward symptoms at least indicate what organs are affected, symptoms like sneezing, coughing, vomiting, diarrhea, and paralysis.

With internal diseases, however, the symptoms are often very vague. The following are typical:
• A sick bird is very quiet.
• Birds that have been rather timid and shy suddenly act surprisingly tame.
• A bird spends much of its time sleeping. When asleep, it does not stand on one leg, the way a healthy bird does, but holds onto the perch with an effort and feet planted apart.
• The plumage is puffed up, the eyes half or tightly shut.
• Breathing may be accelerated, and the beak is often slightly open (see drawing on page 56).
• A sick bird usually loses its appetite and pokes around in the food listlessly with its beak. Sometimes it seems to peck at it eagerly, as though starving, but in actuality it is not eating anything.

The consistency of the droppings isn't a very reliable guide because it depends so much on what the bird has been eating. The normal droppings of a bird consist of two parts: a dark part, which is the actual feces, and a white one, which is the secretion of the kidneys (corresponding to the urine of mammals). The presence of blood, slime, or pus or other obvious deviations from the normal appearance should be interpreted as signs of an illness.

Note: The greenish tinge that may appear after a bird has gone hungry (early in the morning, for instance), is caused by bile and is harmless.

A sick softbill. The plumage of this bird is puffed up as it squats apathetically on its perch, breathing heavily (with open beak) and with feet planted far apart. The eyes remain shut most of the time.

What to Do in Case of Sickness

Minor ailments and injuries can be treated at home, but for anything major a veterinarian should be consulted. Birds are very vulnerable when they are sick, and death is not far away when illness strikes. Veterinary medicine has developed many diagnostic techniques for an exact pinpointing of a disease (for instance, testing for pathogens and measuring their resistance) as well as many medications from which your veterinarian can choose the most appropriate one. Home remedies like camomile tea or infrared radiation alone do not suffice for combating serious infectious and metabolic diseases although they can, like dietary therapy, assist the healing process. Giving medications in the drinking water or in food is often inadequate because the dosage cannot be regulated closely enough; sick birds often eat and drink very little. Particularly at the beginning of treatment, the level of the healing drugs in the blood should stay high. This is most easily accomplished through injections administered by a veterinarian.

Note: Find out in good time, that is, before one of your birds gets sick, where there is a veterinarian familiar with avian medicine and experienced in treating wild as well as caged birds.

First Aid

If you keep a flock of birds, any sick bird should immediately be removed to a quarantine cage. Shine an infrared lamp into one side of the cage for warmth but so that the other part of the cage remains cool. If the sick bird is of a very gregarious species it may be a good idea to move the partner into the same room with the patient, unless the latter is already apathetic. Provide a diet that is easy to digest, such as soft insects with little chitin. In case of light external injuries, bleeding can be controlled by dabbing the wounds with gauze or a cotton swab dipped into ferric chloride. Iodine or any other nonirritating disinfectant can be used to clean wounds, and an antibiotic salve helps to keep out bacteria. Foreign objects (such as thorns) are removed with tweezers. If a wound is open and deep, it should be looked at and stitched by a veterinarian. Broken legs or wings also need the veterinarian's attention.

The Trip to the Veterinarian

For transport, a cardboard box is better than a cage because the bird is better protected in a box. If you do take your bird in a cage, be sure it is well covered. Drive the softbill to the veterinarian in your car if possible; other means of transportation are more upsetting to the bird.

Be prepared to answer the following questions the veterinarian may ask:
• How long has the bird been sick?
• What symptoms have you observed?
• How long have you had the bird?
• Has the bird been sick before? If so, when? What was wrong with it then?
• What treatments has the bird undergone in the past, and what first-aid measures have you taken so far in this instance?

• Has the bird had any contact with newly acquired birds or with wild birds?
• How is the bird housed?
• What do you feed it?
• If the bird is not kept singly, what is the apparent state of health of the others?

Note: Take along a fecal sample of the sick bird; this may save valuable time.

Looking After a Sick Bird

The quarantine cage must be kept in a quiet room that stays evenly warm. The bird should stay there until it is well again. A second fecal analysis and in some instances a final one showing that the bird has completely recovered may be necessary before the patient can be returned to its regular quarters. The floor covering of the quarantine cage should be changed every day, and the perches must be washed frequently and disinfected as needed.

Several days before you plan to let the bird leave the quarantine cage you should start to reduce the use of the heat lamp.

The bird should continue to get easily digestible food and vitamin supplements for a while after recovery. While medication is added to the drinking water, bathing vessels should be removed because the bird will probably prefer the plain water in the bathtub and not get enough of the medicine.

Note: Many birds refuse to touch water to which medication or vitamins have been added. If you do administer medication through the drinking water you should therefore watch your softbill very carefully to make sure it keeps drinking and won't die of thirst.

Relatively Common Disorders

Problems of the Respiratory System

Symptoms: Sneezing or coughing, nasal discharge, abnormal breathing sounds (panting or wheezing), shortness of breath, open-mouth breathing, pronounced tail-bobbing (up-and-down motions of the tail); however, these symptoms are also typical for intestinal disorders (see below).

Causes: Damp and cold surroundings, drafts, infections, fungus infections.

Treatment: In mild cases, keep the bird warm (use an infrared lamp) and feed it easily digestible foods high in vitamins. If a bird is seriously sick, take it to the veterinarian immediately; treatment with antibiotics is necessary.

Inflammation of the Eyes

Symptoms: Red, swollen, or partially pasted together eyelids, continuous tearing, frequent blinking, cloudiness of the eyeball, pussy discharge, sticky lids or feathers around the eyes, frequent eye rubbing, or scratching near the eyes.

Causes: Drafts, foreign objects, infections, vitamin A deficiency, too many mealworms in the diet.

Treatment: Rinse the eyes (with plain tap water, "artificial tears" [available in drugstores], or camomile tea); remove foreign objects if present (use a moistened, cotton-tipped swab); apply an antibiotic eye ointment (but avoid corticosteroids); give a vitamin A supplement; remove sand from cage until the inflammation has cleared up.

Intestinal Problems

Symptoms: The bird sits quietly with puffed-up feathers, sleeps much of the time, and hardly eats anything. The belly is distended; the intestines are full and hard; the feathers around the vent are dirty and sticky; diarrhea.

Causes: Parasites (coccidiae), spoiled food; bacteria (salmonellae, especially in newly acquired birds and in birds kept out of doors), *Escherichia coli,* fungi, viruses, dietary changes, poisons, stress, diseases of other organs, and others.

Treatment: Immediately separate the bird, have a sample dropping analyzed, and initiate the treatment the veterinarian suggests after diagnosis (for instance, antibiotics or sulfonamides); shift to a more easily digestible diet (soft insects), and give the bird weak black tea to drink, and Kaopectate or Pepto-Bismol to soothe and coat the inflamed digestive tract.

Note: Take adequate sanitary measures because some pathogens (such as salmonellae) can also affect humans. Scrub your hands thoroughly after touching the ailing bird or cleaning its cage.

Staggers

Symptoms: The bird is nervous, trembles, twists its head; later, it staggers, has cramps, and tumbles from its perch if agitated.

Causes: Vitamin B or E deficiency; poisoning; virus infection.

Treatment: If the ailment is caused by a nutritional deficiency, add large doses of vitamins to the drinking water until the symptoms disappear completely; prevent recurrence by correcting the bird's diet. If you suspect poisoning, rush the bird to the veterinarian.

Foot Problems

Symptoms: Swellings, inflammations, and wounds on the joints, the soles of the feet, the toes, and often on the eyes as well.

Causes: Faulty living conditions (wrong kind of branches or floor covering); softbills often develop foot problems if they are fed too many mealworms.

Treatment: Correct the environmental factors that may have contributed to the problem. Clean wounds and treat them with antibiotics; move birds temporarily into quarantine cages; supply softer perches (fresh elderberry twigs, for instance); remove sand. Vitamin A therapy.

Note: Preventive care is especially important here because a bird's feet don't heal easily.

Overgrown or Crossed Bill

Symptoms: If the tips of the mandibles grow too long, they tend to cross (see drawing).

A shama with overgrown bill and excessive keratinous growth on its legs. This condition keeps the bird from eating and moving properly. Under improved living conditions such unhealthy developments can be largely avoided.

Causes: Improper environment (the bird has no opportunity to wear down the bill); sometimes a vitamin A deficiency is to blame for this condition, to which shamas are particularly prone.

Treatment: With sharp scissors or nail clippers cut the tips of the overgrown bill back to proper size; try to re-create the original shape of the bill, or it will become more and more deformed. Make sure you don't injure the mandible when trimming it. A coating of glycerin helps keep the horn on the bill from cracking. If bleeding should occur, apply ferric chloride.

Caution: Only very experienced aviculturists should attempt to correct the shape of a bird's bill. An injured beak may mean that your softbill is condemned to starve to death. If you have the slightest doubt about your abilities, take the bird to an experienced pet dealer or to the veterinarian!

Health Care and List of Diseases

Excessive Formation of Keratin on the Legs

Symptoms: Thickening of the horny layer on the bird's legs and feet; this affects primarily older softbills (see drawing on page 58).

Causes: Old age; insufficient wear; possibly a vitamin A deficiency.

Treatment: Soften the horn on the legs with a salicylic acid ointment, Vaseline, or an antibiotic salve, then remove the excess horn carefully to prevent inflammation.

Prevention: Keep the birds in a well-planted aviary that offers condition resembling those in nature; leg bands help wear down the horn through friction.

Fractures

Symptoms: Abnormal posture of the leg or wing; with compound fractures, bleeding.

Causes: See Dangers (page 29–31).

Treatment: Ordinarily, broken bones heal quickly in birds (in about 2 weeks). A broken leg should be put in a splint (as in a drinking straw that has been slit open). In case of a broken femur the leg should be immobilized against the body. A broken wing is taped to the body in normal rest position. Only a very experienced aviculturist should attempt to perform these treatments. If you have the slightest question about your competency, take the bird to the veterinarian specializing in birds. If the fracture is compound or if some tissue is already dead, a visit to the veterinarian is mandatory. Keep the bird in a small cage while the fracture is healing. If the wing is bandaged, the bird should not be able to hop or climb higher than a couple of inches (danger of tumbling to the ground!).

Overgrown Claws

Symptoms: Very long toenails that may start to curl in corkscrew fashion. The nails interfere with landing on perches and become entangled in nesting materials, the wire grating of the cage, and similar objects.

Cause: Insufficient wear of the nails because of inappropriate perches (too thin or too smooth).

Treatment: Trim the nails with sharp scissors or nail clippers. Be careful not to cut into blood vessels (these can be seen in light-colored claws). If you do draw blood, apply cotton with ferric chloride or stick the bleeding claw into a bar of plain soap.

Prevention: Supply natural branches.

Egg Binding

Symptoms: The female squats on the ground with raised feathers, breathes hard, and intermittently strains hard. The abdomen is bloated, red, and hot. Usually you can feel the egg above the cloaca, and sometimes it is even visible in the cloaca.

Causes: This may be the female's first egg; she may be too young or too fat; or she may have laid too many eggs. The eggs may be deformed or soft-shelled, or the bird may be suffering from an inflammation of the oviduct.

Treatment: This condition requires immediate attention, preferably from an avian veterinarian, or death will follow promptly. If you cannot take the bird to the veterinarian, expose her underside to warm steam (in the quarantine cage and using an infrared lamp); massage the abdomen gently, and try giving an enema of cod-liver oil, paraffin oil, or vegetable oil.

Prevention: A diet that is high in vitamins and calcium.

Abnormal Molt

Symptoms: The bird fails to molt at the proper time, or only part of the plumage is replaced; there may be bald spots where new feathers grow in only reluctantly or not at all. Changes in the pigmentation (dilution or darkening of color).

Causes: Improper living conditions, such as frequent interruptions of the daily routine, wrong temperature (usually too warm); insufficient light; poor diet (undersupply of some nutrients or oversupply of calories); too little exercise.

Treatment: Remedy the situation giving rise to the problem; add vitamin, mineral, and amino acid supplements to the food or drinking water. A diet high in protein together with regular exposure to an infrared lamp often helps to get the molt started.

Parasites

Coccidia

Symptoms: General decline, ruffled plumage, loss of weight, diarrhea (may be mixed with blood or slime); sometimes death.

Cause: Protozoans in the lining of the intestines. These produce oocysts (a form of egg) that are excreted in the droppings and picked up by the other birds when they peck for food. Oocysts can accumulate on the cage or aviary floor and cause rapid spreading of a disease in the flock. Latent infections often break out with full force when the birds' natural resistance is weakened because of inappropriate living conditions, inadequate food, other infections, or stress. Newly acquired birds are often infested.

Treatment: When the presence of coccidia is revealed, the entire flock must be treated. After diagnosis by the veterinarian, drugs against coccidia are added to the drinking water. Various medications work differently, so it is important to follow the veterinarian's directions exactly. The cure is usually successful, but strict hygiene is required to prevent reinfection.

Regular fecal examinations help the aviculturist detect dangerous buildups of the parasites in time.

Worms in the Gastrointestinal Tract

Symptoms: There are few unmistakable signs. The birds are usually listless and lose weight; the plumage is puffed up, and eventually they get diarrhea.

Causes: Parasites such as tapeworms, roundworms, and threadworms infest the digestive system. The worm eggs are swallowed either directly or in their intermediary hosts (insects the birds eat).

Treatment: After the veterinarian has determined that there are worm eggs or sections of tapeworm in the droppings, the entire flock must be treated with the right worming medicine, which is added to the drinking water. Sometimes the birds must be wormed a second time to get rid of the generation of worms that develops from eggs.

Worms in the Respiratory System (Gapeworms)

Symptoms: Coughing, retching, yawning, intermittent severe or minor breathing difficulties.

Cause: Small, red worms in the breathing tubes. Male worms measuring only a few millimeters are attached to the females, which measure almost an inch (2 cm). Eggs that are coughed up are swallowed and excreted. Then they are often eaten by earthworms or snails and slugs. If the birds eat these, the gapeworms end up inside the birds again. Direct infection without intermediary hosts also occurs. Gapeworms multiply especially quickly during spells of wet weather; dry weather and the sun tend to destroy the eggs.

Treatment: Treatment (usually with thiabenzole) is difficult and should be administered by a veterinarian.

Prevention: Very important! Clean the cage floor daily; in an aviary, keep the ground dry. Try to keep wild birds away by roofing over the aviary. Don't feed the birds earthworms or mollusks. Watch the birds for signs of breathing difficulty (breathing with open beak or "gaping").

Red Mites, also Called Feather Mites

Symptoms: The birds are restless at night; anemia; weakness; death, particularly in nestlings.

Cause: Blood-sucking mites that hide during the day in cracks, nests, and litter. At night they suck the birds' blood.

Treatment: Examine cracks, corners, wooden boards, perches, and other hiding places minutely with a magnifying glass for mites. If the inside walls of a box cage are painted white, red mites, which are about the size of the head of a pin, are easy to see at night. Combat them with insecticides containing pyrethrin or cabaryl. (Follow the instructions carefully!) Dust the birds with powder, and paint infested cage accessories with a watery solution. After this treatment, the accessories must be thoroughly scrubbed. Aerosol should not be used on softbills or in their presence (danger of poisoning!).

Prevention: Check the cage carefully and regularly for signs of red mites; burn old nests, and never use nests of wild birds.

Fungi
Molds

Symptoms: There are no unmistakable signs. Affected birds have difficulty breathing or generally do not feel well; eventually they may suffocate.

Cause: Molds are everywhere. A healthy organism usually has sufficient resistance and succumbs to them only if its defenses are weakened by stress, illness, the strain of becoming acclimated to a new home, improper housing, or an inadequate diet. The molds spread primarily over the mucous membranes of the respiratory system. An exact diagnosis is difficult.

Treatment: The treatment is determined by a veterinarian and its success is far from assured.

Yeasts (Thrush, Candidiasis, Moniliasis)

Symptoms: The infected bird has difficulty eating and breathing; it chokes up slime, and there is a white coating on the mucous membranes inside the beak.

Causes: Yeast fungi are present everywhere. When a bird's resistance is lowered or if it has a vitamin A deficiency, the fungi can cause sickness. Softbills living on fruit and nectar are especially susceptible because leftover bits of their sticky food provide an ideal breeding ground for the yeast.

Treatment: This condition must be treated by a veterinarian; chances for a cure are good.

Rickets and Osteomalacia

Symptoms: Rickets affects immature birds; osteomalacia, older ones. These conditions manifest themselves in bent bones, deformed limbs, and a tendency to break bones.

Causes: Vitamin D deficiency and lack of calcium.

Treatment: Increased doses of vitamin D (vitamin D_3 is especially important) and calcium (in the form of a vitamin and mineral supplement), which are added to the food; also exposure to direct sunlight or ultraviolet rays. Limbs that are already misshapen cannot be corrected.

Poisoning

Symptoms: These vary depending on the poisoning agent. Some of the symptoms are general ill health, breathing difficulties, diarrhea, apathy, fits of agitation, and death. A single bird or an entire flock can be affected.

Causes: These too can vary. Some examples are disinfectants, poisonous plants, glues, environmental poisons present in food insects, and sprays against such parasites as mites.

Treatment: Try to alleviate the symptoms and, if necessary, consult the veterinarian. Remove the cause. General measures that usually help are warmth, fresh air, easily digestible food, and vitamins. Cut off feathers smeared with glue; don't try to clean them with acetone or gasoline.

Interesting Facts About Softbills

All the softbills discussed in this book are essentially wild birds. In contrast to domesticated birds (such as chickens, domestic pigeons, canaries, and parakeets), which are so used to living under human care that many could no longer survive on their own, caged softbills exhibit the same characteristics and variety of behavior typical of their wild cousins, even if they have been bred in captivity for two or three generations. Keeping and breeding wild birds is considerably more demanding than keeping and raising domesticated ones. Their requirements for nesting sites are more stringent; courtship must proceed without interruptions and distractions in order to culminate in a successful union; and for rearing their young the birds need live food that resembles the prey they find in the wild. This is true even if they have been eating a substitute diet happily all along. Your ability to provide what your birds need to thrive will increase as you learn more about their biology.

Flying Ability and Body Structure

In most birds, the entire body is modified to increase flying efficiency. Exterior shape, skeleton, muscles, circulation, and metabolism are all adapted to the exigencies of flight.

- A bird's bones are very light, and many of them have air sacs inside them.
- The body shape conforms to aerodynamic principles. This is achieved in part by the fusion of some bones of the body so that they form a solid "fuselage" and by the plumage.
- Instead of forelimbs, birds have wings that are moved by powerful pectoral muscles.
- The lungs permit the intake of oxygen during both inhaling and exhaling.
- A relatively large heart, blood that is richer in red blood corpuscles than that of mammals, a very fast pulse and breathing rate, and a body temperature higher than that of other creatures all contribute to the enormous energy a bird needs to fly.

- The absence of teeth, a vestigial right ovary, and the ability to form eggs very rapidly (within 1 day) help reduce body weight so that the wings can be built all the more powerfully.
- Even a bird's eating habits are subordinate to the principle of flight efficiency. Most birds eat a diet low in fiber and high in proteins and carbohydrates, nutrients that can be quickly digested. Their intestines are not filled with food that breaks down slowly like those of ruminants, for example. This means, of course, that birds need to eat almost constantly. Hunger and thirst, even for relatively short periods, are deadly for most birds.

The Feathers

The feathers of a bird regulate its body temperature, contribute to its streamlined shape, serve as carrying surfaces and steering devices, and also have camouflage and signaling functions. Although the entire bird is clothed in them with hardly any gaps, the feathers are not distributed evenly and grow only in certain places, the so-called feather tracts. Feathers are complex structures made of a horny substance. We distinguish between two main types of feathers: contour feathers and down feathers.

Contour Feathers: These determine the external appearance of a bird. They come in two sizes: the short contour feathers, which cover the body, and the long flight feathers of the wings and tail.

At the center of a feather is a stiff, tapering shaft, the rachis, from which grow the distal (away from the body) and proximal (close to the body) vanes. The vanes are made up of many parallel rows of rods, or barbs. These in turn carry minute barbules equipped with tiny hooks on one side that lock into grooves on the adjacent side of the next barbule, working on the same principle as a zipper. The result is a continuous, solid, yet elastic surface.

Down Feathers: The down feathers are concealed under the contour feathers. They lack bar-

Interesting Facts About Softbills

A sleeping mynah. Unlike most other passerines, the mynah doesn't tuck its head into the back feathers but hunches it down between the shoulders.

bules and are loose and soft. Their main function is to keep the body warm.

Molt: Since feathers are made up of dead tissue and deteriorate with time, they are replaced periodically. This happens at certain seasons, primarily at the end of the reproductive cycle. In some species the molt occurs in several stages. After the softbills coming from other parts of the world have adjusted to our seasons, they usually molt in the late summer or in the fall like our native birds. The molting process is regulated by hormones and affected by factors like light, temperature, and nutrition.

Molt Caused by Fright: If you catch a bird and it is severely frightened, it may unexpectedly shed its tail feathers or some of its contour feathers. This is not caused by sickness but by a protective mechanism. In the wild, a predator would be left with a mouthful of feathers instead of the whole bird. The feathers, of course, are quickly replaced in a healthy bird.

Feather Colors: The coloration of the plumage serves as camouflage and as a signal for the recognition of sex and species. Many striking markings function as keys that trigger certain instinctive responses during the reproductive cycle. The color of a bird's feathers is produced both by color pigments and by structural features of the feather. Yellows and reds result primarily from fat-soluble carotenoid or lipochrome pigments. Other colors,

such as blue, white, and some blacks, are not produced by pigments but by microscopic, light-refracting structures in the feathers. These are called structural colors.

Sometimes caged birds exhibit color alterations caused by the conditions of captivity.

Bleaching of color occurs with some frequency in birds that have bright green, yellow, or red areas in the plumage. The fading of the colors starts when the bird molts. The problem is associated mostly with pigments of the carotenoid group.

These pigments originate at least partly in food and are deposited in the growing feathers. If the food is low in carotene, there is not enough pigment for the newly forming feathers. Sometimes a deficiency in certain fats also plays a role because fats are needed for the absorption of carotenoids by the organism. A bird that is losing its natural coloration does not turn all white; instead, its plumage takes on the hues that the remaining coloring agents permit. (In Pekin robins, white-eyes, and leafbirds, yellow feathers may pale and green ones turn a bluish gray.) This discoloration is not a sickness per se, but it should nevertheless be regarded as a sign that the conditions of captivity are less than perfect.

Remedy: Food high in carotene (before and

Red-eared bulbuls. The slightly hunched posture and the flattened crest indicate some anxiety.

63

during the molt) and increased exercise (to stimulate circulation) can counteract the fading and even reverse it. Once you have corrected the conditions that gave rise to the problem, the new feathers growing in after the next molt should exhibit the original strong colors. Pet stores also sell synthetic carotene supplements that are added to the food and help maintain the natural colors.

Sensory Organs

Birds find their way around in the world primarily through the use of their eyes and ears.

The eyes of most birds are disproportionately large compared with their body size. Because they are on the side of the head, birds have an extremely wide angle of vision, sometimes up to or even exceeding a radius of 300 degrees. The area that lies within the range of both eyes and where the vision is three-dimensional is much smaller, often less than 25 degrees. When a softbill wants to scrutinize something, it does so by turning its head sideways and peering with one eye (as when contemplating the food dish; see drawing on page 36). In contrast to most mammals, which close their eyes by lowering the upper eyelid, birds raise the lower lid. They also have a third, inner lid, the so-called nictitating membrane, which can be drawn over the cornea underneath the lids.

The hearing of birds is excellent. Their ears resemble those of other vertebrates although there is no external ear and the entire structure is hidden underneath the feathers. The feathers of the auricular region lack barbules (see page 62) so that they don't interfere with the sound waves. A bird's range of hearing is comparable to that of humans, although apparently birds can distinguish considerably shorter sound sequences than people can.

The sense of smell is of only minor importance for most birds.

The sense of taste is often underestimated in birds. Softbills, especially those that live primarily on fruit and nectar, have quite a well-developed sense of taste. This is one of the reasons that some of them react so strongly to medications in their food and drinking water.

Important Patterns of Behavior

In this section only those areas of behavior that are of special importance in keeping softbills are discussed.

Singing

Birds have a large and varied repertoire of sound utterances. Their voices don't originate in the larynx, as do those of mammals, but in the syrinx, a vocal organ that resembles the larynx but is located farther down in the trachea where the bronchi branch off. The syrinx consists of modified cartilage rings in the upper bronchi and in some species in the lower trachea as well. A special muscle system manipulates the shape of the syrinx, setting the air that is exhaled vibrating at different frequencies and thus producing a variety of tones and pitches.

In addition to actual song, birds have other vocal expressions, such as calling, hissing, luring, and begging sounds, all of which have specific functions in the life of a bird. Some of these functions have to do with claiming and defending territory, finding mates, ensuring flock cohesion, and individual recognition. There also seems to be considerable evidence that in many species (like robins and shamas) some song is indulged in for its own sake, without purpose or motive beyond the mere pleasure of singing.

Male and female birds share some vocal expressions and differ in others. What is properly described as song is usually the domain of the male. In many species the females sing as well, however, and in some the two partners sing simultaneously, producing "duets."

Many songs and most call notes are inborn, but

Interesting Facts About Softbills

A male shama in courtship mood. With erect body and with the tail pointing straight up, he is ready to embark on his courtship song, the so-called motif song.

others must be learned from either the male parent or another member of the flock. Some species are capable of learning new songs as long as they live, a trait that is often combined with the ability to incorporate alien sounds into their own songs. The mocking of shamas and of gold-fronted leafbirds is an example of this, as is the talent for human speech that mynahs and parrots display. We know very little about the biologic reasons for sound imitation in birds. Birds differ not only in what they imitate; each bird also has its own unique voice although the differences between individual voices are practically indistinguishable to our ears. Birds of the same species but from a different background even speak in different "dialects."

Aggression

Aggression includes threatening and attack behavior as well as defense. It is obviously necessary for the survival of individual birds, but its role may be even more crucial for the peaceful coexistence of birds of the same species as well as of different species (for instance in establishing rank order and defining territory). Aggression can be directed against a member of the species or against any other creature.

A conflict in nature usually ends with the weaker party being routed or openly admitting defeat by displaying a gesture of submission. In a cage or aviary, however, fights can have fatal consequences. There is not enough room for flight, and gestures of submission lose their effectiveness because the mere continued presence of the offending party keeps evoking aggression in the dominant bird. In addition, a gesture of submission may not be recognized as such by an opponent that belongs to a different species. It is best, therefore, to prevent conflicts as much as possible by combining the right kinds of birds and by paying attention to different requirements for housing (see page 24).

Social Behavior

Some softbills (like the shamas) live completely solitary lives except during the mating season. Others (white-eyes and Pekin robins) live together in flocks (and sometimes with other species of similar habits) except when breeding. They split up into pairs only to raise their young. There are even softbills that don't mind the presence of other members of their own species near their nests and in fact breed in colonies (mynahs and starlings).

Social softbills should be kept in pairs or — outside the mating season — in flocks. In the absence of others of the same species, different softbills can be combined in a flock, as long as all of them are equally sociable.

The typical behavior of social birds includes mutual preening, in which two partners take turns grooming each other's feathers, particularly in the

Interesting Facts About Softbills

head region. In the course of this grooming, dirt, feather particles, left-over feather sheaths, and parasites are removed. Mutual preening serves not only practical ends, however; it also strengthens the pair bond. The members of some social species are nevertheless quick to respond to each other aggressively (white-eyes, for instance), and here the mutual preening takes on the quality of a gesture of

Social preening. Two white-eyes are preening a third one, which shows its contentment by raising its throat feathers.

submission. The attacked bird holds out the raised plumage of its neck to the aggressor, and the latter can't help but groom it (see drawing).

The need for physical contact is so great in some social species that a single bird will seek a companion with similar behavior patterns from another species, disregarding differences in size and dissimilarity of biologic family. Examples of such misalliances that I have seen include the union of a white-eye and a Pekin robin and another of a white-eye and a lavender waxbill (an exotic finch). The latter two birds learned to recognize each other by voice and built a nest together.

Sleeping

Most softbills sleep in the branches of trees or bushes. Mynahs, however, like to spend the night in an enclosed cavity. Almost all softbills sleep resting on one leg. A special arrangement of the

tendons makes the toes grip the perch tightly when the muscles relax so the bird does not fall off during sleep. The head is tucked into the back feathers (see drawing). Mynahs are an exception here, too; they merely hunch the head down between the shoulders with the beak pointing straight ahead (see drawing on page 63). Many social birds (white-eyes and Pekin robins, for example) sleep in colonies. They huddle so closely together that the silhouette of a pair looks much like a single bird with two tails. In these species even unmated birds sleep perched together, looking like a row of fluffy cotton balls stuck on a branch.

A sleeping pair of Pekin robins. Like many other social birds, Pekin robins nestle together to sleep and tuck their bills into their back feathers.

Birds belonging to solitary species, on the other hand, avoid physical contact. Even for sleeping they keep at a safe distance from each other, leaving enough space to be out of reach of any neighbor's beak.

Comfort Behavior

This term is used to describe such behavior as individual and mutual preening, bathing in water (see drawing on page 9) and in sand, and sunbathing (see drawing on page 24).

There is one form of comfort behavior that many birds in the wild enjoy but that most of our captive softbills must do without. Birds sometimes deliberately let ants crawl all over them or rub them into their feathers with the beak. This is called "anting." Birds probably do it to get rid of external parasites and perhaps also of old dry skin. If there are ants' nests near your birds' outdoor aviary you might keep an eye out for this form of behavior.

Life Expectancy

Songbirds may live 10 years or even longer. In nature very few reach such an age. The chance of surviving the first year is only about 25 to 30 percent for songbirds, and after that an array of dangers, disease, and harsh living conditions keep claiming victims. The average life span of birds living in captivity is much greater because famine and predators are eliminated and many diseases can be cured. The following instances of longevity have been recorded: A shama lived to age 26, an Oriental white-eye lived over 23 years, and a white-cheeked bulbul reached age 13. In these cases the recorded age includes only the time the birds spent in captivity; their actual age was therefore even higher.

Descriptions of Popular Softbills

In the following pages we introduce softbills that are frequently kept in cages and aviaries and that are more or less regularly available from pet dealers. They are all birds that can do well in a cage or aviary.

The descriptions of the individual species include information about origin, appearance, behavior, and song, as well as specific advice regarding the birds' demands in captivitiy.

The sizes given for the birds refer to the overall length of an adult, measured from the tip of the beak to the end of the tail. In the scientific (Latin or Greek) names, the first word stands for the genus and the second for the species; a third term indicates a subspecies.

Protection of Endangered Species

Our time is witnessing a frightening decline in the number of plants and animals on this earth. Many species are already extinct or are threatened, worldwide or regionally, with immediate extinction. There are many and complex causes for this, but the ongoing destruction of habitat and changes in biotopes are the major villains.

Bird fanciers and aviculturists have a chance to play a significant role in helping to preserve some of the variety of bird life by maintaining and perhaps even helping to increase the populations of some species.

In an attempt to protect threatened animals and plants worldwide, the Convention on International Trade in Endangered Species of Wild Fauna and Flora was drawn up and signed in Washington in 1973. This document is generally referred to by the acronym CITES and contains three appendices in which endangered species are listed according to the degree of seriousness with which their survival is threatened. The appendices are revised and updated periodically to reflect the newest population findings.

Current regulations concerning the importation of birds into the United States may be found on pages 97–99.

The Timaliidae Family (Babblers)

The Timaliidae family includes many different and different-looking birds from Africa, Asia, Australia, and the islands surrounding those regions, as well as one species that lives in North America. The greatest number of species occurs in Southeast Asia. The Timaliidae display a greater variety of shape, size, and color than just about any other family in the order of Passeriformes or passerines (perching songbirds). Some members of the family resemble wrens or chickadees; others, Old World warblers or flycatchers; and others yet, thrushes or even jays. Many Timaliidae are very colorful, some are excellent singers, and some combine both these qualities. It is no wonder that a number of these birds are very popular cagebirds. The Pekin robin, the silver-eared mesia, its red subspecies *Leiothrix argentauris laurinus*, and the blue-winged siva are obvious examples.

Pekin Robin
(Other popular names: Pekin nightingale, red-billed nightingale, Japanese nightingale, Chinese nightingale)
Leiothrix lutea (Scopoli, 1786)

68

Descriptions of Popular Softbills

Photos on front cover and page 27.
Drawings on pages 10, 24, and 66.

Distribution: The Himalayan area from Kashmir in the west to Assam in the southeast; western and northeastern Burma and northern Tonkin; from southern China northward to Szechwan and southern Shensi and eastward to the Yangtse River estuary. The Pekin robin has also been introduced to some of the Hawaiian Islands. *Habitat:* Underbrush of mountain forests, land with brushy and grassy vegetation, and plantations. *Overall length:* 6 to 6¼ inches (15–15.5 cm). *Appearance:* Only minor differences between the sexes; the colors are somewhat muted in the female with the white cross-bar on the upper side of the tail either lacking or very faint. *Behavior:* The birds usually stay close to the ground, where they hunt for insects. Outside the breeding season they are gregarious, roaming through their hunting territory in small flocks that may include other species. They generally live in pairs during the breeding season. *Voice:* The males and females have different characteristic call notes; the males also sing well. The song is loud and pleasant. *Names:* All the popular names of this species are misleading; the Pekin robin is neither a robin nor a nightingale. Its song is quite different from that of nightingales, too.

Requirements in Captivity

Pekin robins are not demanding about their food and can therefore be recommended for someone who is just starting out with softbills. Males in particular are available at pet stores year-round. However, these gregarious birds should be kept only in pairs. They can also be combined with other species. Pekin robins become tame quickly even if they live in pairs.

Housing: Pekin robins enjoy flying and moving about, and their quarters should therefore be of generous dimensions.

Cage: If you plan to keep your birds in a cage, buy one that exceeds the minimum measurements given on page 12 quite a bit. In a small cage these birds can only run through the same limited sequence of movements over and over again. Pekin robins need at least an hour of flying freely in the room in addition to the exercise they get in the cage. Since they live in the underbrush in nature, they will spend most of their time in the lower half of a room (among the table and chair legs); they will also be happy among flowering houseplants or plants in the window.

Indoor aviary: An indoor aviary is preferable to a cage because it gives the birds more freedom of movement.

Outdoor aviary: The aviary should be densely planted. Since Pekin robins live in mountain forests as high as 9000 feet (2700 m) above sea level, they adapt quite well to our temperate climate and can spend most of the year in an outdoor aviary. During winter weather, however, they must have access to a shelter where the temperature does not drop below freezing.

Feeding: Pekin robins are not very fussy eaters. They consume both commercial insect food and fruit. In addition to these staples they gratefully accept live insects, spiders, millipedes, and other arthropods. Many Pekin robins round out their diet with foods like chick pellets, mynah pellets, dog food, and even dry or sprouted grains (millet and rolled hemp seed). Some like to take a sip of nectar drink now and then.

Note: The plumage of caged Pekin robins tends to fade gradually (see page 63). This is especially true of the dark green parts on the head and back, which turn a pale blue. If this happens, make sure you supply a diet extra rich in carotene and provide more exercise.

Disposition: Pekin robins are extremely gregarious birds whose pleasant nature becomes fully evident only if they are kept in pairs. A pair of Pekin robins spend much of the day preening each other and sleep nestled closely together, looking like a single ball of fluff. When flying freely in the room or roaming around the aviary, the two partners almost always keep within sight of each other or maintain at least vocal contact. Any excursion is frequently interrupted by a few moments of cuddling together.

Voice: The song of the male resembles that of the blue gray gnatcatcher (Polioptila caerulea), but it is not as varied and rich in motifs as the song of a shama (see page 71) or of a gold-fronted leafbird (see page 82). In addition to songs and alarm calls, Pekin robins utter a number of other calls that serve to maintain contact between the birds when they move about in thick brush. These contact calls vary between males and females and can help in identifying the sex of a bird. Catch the bird whose sex you are trying to determine and remove it from the flock, housing it where it can still hear its companions. You will be able to tell whether it is a cock or a hen immediately by its calls. The contact call of a male is like a softly sung phrase of a song, whereas the female emits a series of two to three plaintive notes.

Breeding

Pekin robins and shamas are the softbills most commonly bred in captivity.

Nest: In nature, Pekin robins weave cup-shaped nests in the crotch of a branch. In a cage or aviary, they often attempt to do the same, but the nests they build are often not solid enough for lack of appropriate nesting materials. You can make life easier for your birds by placing a bowl-shaped nest basket where the birds are starting to build. Most birds accept the basket as a base for their nest. Coconut fibers and sisal are good weaving materials.

Rearing the Young: Parent birds almost always want live insects for feeding their young. Sometimes they accept freshly killed or frozen insects. If the birds are well acclimated to an outdoor aviary in a garden, you can let them fly freely as long as the nestlings are still nest-bound, so that they can catch live insects on their own (see page 51). Continue giving the birds their usual soft food, together with berries and fruit rich in vitamins, in addition to the fresh insects. This way they will get an optimal diet, and the youngsters will adjust to commercial food easily. You can keep the entire family together in an aviary until the original pair enters a new mating cycle. At that point you should remove the younger generation so that the parents can proceed with their mating undisturbed.

Singing Lessons: Young cocks develop into accomplished singers only if they have a good teacher. Otherwise their song remains quite amateurish. To improve their musicality, you should play tapes of good singers to them as much as you can. It's never too late to do this. Pekin robin cocks are capable of learning new songs and refining their voices even after they are fully mature.

Breeding Data

Nesting sites in nature: In bushes and other dense cover no more than about 2 to 6 feet (0.5–1.5 m) above ground.
Incubation and nestling care: Males and females take turns sitting on the nest and feeding the nestlings.
Clutch: Three to four conical eggs that are very wide at one end and very pointed at the other; they are pale green with gray and reddish brown spots, particularly at the wide end. Size of eggs: 22 × 16 mm.
Incubation period: 12 to 13 days.
Nestling period: 11 to 13 days.

Related Species

Silver-eared Mesia

Leiothrix argentauris (Hodgson, 1837)
Photos on page 28 and on back cover

Distribution: From the Himalayas (about as far west as the 79th degree of longitude) eastward across Assam to southern China; northern Indochina; from Burma and northwestern Thailand south as far as Malaysia and western Sumatra. *Habitat:* The same as Pekin robin. *Overall length:* 6½ inches (17 cm). *Appearance and disposition:* The silver-eared mesia differs from the Pekin robin in having an extensive black cap and light cheeks. The tail coverts are red in the male and ocher colored in the female. In behavior the silver-eared mesia resembles the Pekin robin. *Requirements in captivity:* Essentially the same as for the Pekin robin, but this species prefers a higher proportion of insects in its diet. Silver-eared mesias are considered somewhat more delicate than Pekin robins and do better in an aviary than a cage. *Voice:* The song is similar to that of the Pekin robin but louder and more monotonous.

Red Silver-eared Mesia

L. argentauris laurinus (subspecies)

This bird is larger and even more colorful than the silver-eared mesia. In the subspecies from Sumatra both sexes have some red feathers (see photo on page 28). More commonly available at pet stores than this subspecies from Sumatra is one from South China, in which only the male is partially red. Both these subspecies should be kept only by experienced bird fanciers.

Blue-winged Siva

Siva cyanouroptera (Hodgson, 1837)
Photo on page 27

Distribution: In the Himalayas about as far west as the 79th degree of longitude; in China to Szechwan, eastern Kuwangsi and Hainan; in Indochina, parts of Burma and Thailand, and in Malaysia. *Habitat:* Underbrush or forests, bamboo thickets, and plantations. *Overall length:* 5½ inches (14 cm). *Appearance and disposition:* The plumage is less showy than that of the Pekin robin. Both sexes look alike. Blue-winged sivas are charming, lively birds. *Requirements in captivity:* The same as for Pekin robins. *Voice:* Pleasant; softer than Pekin robins.

The Muscicapidae Family (Flycatchers)

This family has a very wide distribution, members of it being found in almost all inhabitable parts of the earth. Muscicapidae have adapted to the most varied environments, from inhospitable tundras and high mountains to jungles and rain forests. They range from polar regions to the tropics. Many species prefer living close to the ground.

Over 420 species are included in the Muscicapidae family, and the birds consequently display a great variety of shapes and colors. The family can be roughly subdivided into two groups. One group, sometimes called the chat-thrushes, takes in the slenderer thrushlike birds (for example, European nightingales, the bluebirds, and various flycatchers). Of the softbills discussed in this book it includes the shama, the dayal, and the snowy-headed robin chat. The second group, the true or typical thrushes, are stouter birds, such as the dama thrush and the robin. Males and females of both groups may have the same coloration (wood thrush and veery, for example) or be clearly dimorphic in size and color (the shama). The juveniles of most Muscicapidae are brownish with darker spots. Many species have musical voices, and some are among the most talented singers of the bird world.

Shama

(Also called shama thrush; sometimes the name magpie robin is used for birds of the *Copsychus* genus)
Copsychus malabaricus (Scopoli, 1788)
Photos on page 46 and on back cover
Drawings on pages 36, 58, and 65

Distribution: India and Indochina, the Andaman Islands, Southern China, islands of Indonesia; has also been introduced to Hawaii. *Habitat:* Jungles in lowlands and in hilly country, often near water. *Overall length and appearance:* Male: 9¾ to 11 inches (25–28 cm), almost two-thirds of which is made up of the tail. Upper side bluish black. The female is somewhat smaller with a shorter tail. She is ash gray on top, and the chestnut brown on the underside is more muted. The juveniles resemble the female. *Behavior:* Shamas are strictly territorial and, except during the mating season, solitary. They forage mostly along the ground for insects, spiders, worms, snails, and other small creatures. *Voice:* The shama is considered one of the best songbirds anywhere to be found. Its song is loud, mellifluous, and varied. Shamas are also outstanding mimics. The female sings too. When excited or

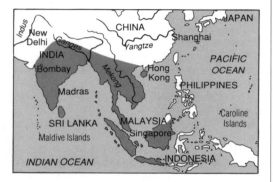

alarmed the birds utter a sharp tock-tock. *Name:* Although the name shama thrush is often used, this bird is not a true thrush.

Requirements in Captivity

The shama has many qualities that make it an ideal cage bird: its requirements are modest; it becomes tame quickly; it has a lively temperament and an attractive appearance; it sings readily and its song is varied; and it lives long. A shama is a particularly good choice if you don't want to have more than one bird. Since it is solitary by nature it misses the company of its fellows less than more gregarious softbills do.

Housing: Since shamas don't get along well together you can keep a pair only in a large aviary. Keeping more than one male in the same space is impossible.

Cage: Shamas have impressively long tails and therefore need a large cage (see Minimum Dimensions, page 12). A box cage placed where the light is not too bright suits them well. It gives them a

sense of security, which they need because in nature they are used to the cover of dense vegetation, and it also minimizes the amount of sand and left-over food that gets kicked out into the room.

The cage should have only a few branches for perching on. Because this bird spends much of its time on the ground you should put a few rocks, a piece of a thick branch, or some similar object in the bottom of the cage to give the bird something to do. Food and water dishes are also placed on the floor, in a spot where they are safe from droppings. Some shamas refuse to bathe in an enclosed bathhouse. If this is the case with your bird, put a dish with water on the floor when the shama flies freely in the room. Generally, the birds welcome this opportunity. A bowl with fresh moss, some sod, or some leaf mold will keep your bird happy and occupied and at the same time provides additional minerals and food (arthropods and worms).

Note: Many shamas suffer from overgrown beaks in captivity (see page 58). A bowl with fresh earth gives them a chance to wear off some of the excess horn as they poke around in the earth.

Indoor aviary: This provides a more suitable home for these large birds. The same rules apply for setting it up as for a cage.

Outdoor aviary: During the summer a shama can be kept outdoors. Since its original home is in the tropics or subtropics, however, it needs heated quarters during winter. Some shamas live together peacefully with other kinds of birds, but some do not.

Feeding: Shamas are easy to please. Commercial insect food (preferably with fat) is a fine staple but should be complemented by additional foods, such as hard-boiled egg and ant pupae. Many shamas like mynah pellets, chickfeed in pellet form, or softened dog food. Shamas are also crazy about mealworms, but they shouldn't get more than 10 to 15 per day. You can be more generous with other, less fatty insects (crickets, millipedes, wood lice, small spiders, and grubs). Berries and small pieces of fruit are another excellent addition to the diet but are not always accepted. Small portions of finely chopped chickweed, cress, or lettuce leaves should be mixed into the regular food every day. If your shamas are raising young, they need live insects.

Note: Some indigestible elements in the food (as in insects with a lot of chitin) are important for a shama's well-being; the birds routinely spit out the indigestible parts in the form of small balls.

Disposition: Shamas become tame quickly and soon develop a close relationship with their keepers. After flying freely in the room they can easily be lured back to their cage with a mealworm.

Note: Caution! When loose in a room, shamas spend much of their time on the floor, and if they are tame they can easily be stepped on because they don't know enough to get out of the way.

Voice: The shama's song is highly musical, composed of manyvaried motifs, and includes much mimicking. The motifs are continuously altered and varied through the incorporation of new sounds and other bird voices. The song can be broken down into three basic types:
• loud song composed of motifs (its primary purpose is the establishment of territory and pair formation)
• soft aggressive song (used in defending territory and in initiating pair formation)
• resting song, which can go on for over an hour without a break

These types of song are accompanied by different stances. In the motif song, the bird sits straight up and angles the tail high; the aggressive song is performed with spread wings and fanned tail; and for the resting song the birds adopt a relaxed posture with lightly puffed feathers.

The females sing too, but less often and with shorter songs. The two partners of a mating pair pick up each other's themes and incorporate them in their responses. Since hearing an imitation of their own song triggers aggression in shamas, entire sections of a partner's song are repeated only if the pair have lost sight of each other; it's almost like calling the mate by name. Not all shamas sing equally well. Lack of enthusiasm for singing is often due to imperfect living conditions (inappro-

priate cage location; irregular days; one-sided, overly rich, or inadequate food). The first thing to do, if your shama is reluctant to sing, is to review whether all its needs are being met. Shamas never lose their ability to learn and can easily be induced to sing, perhaps by having tapes of other birds or of music played.

Note: Two shama cocks can stimulate each other to sing or can complement each other's songs, but only if their cages are not too close (put them in adjacent rooms). If they are too near each other, their singing often turns into a brief and violent contest with the distressing result that the loser will never sing another note.

Breeding

Shamas are one kind of softbill that is bred regularly in captivity. They are most likely to reproduce in a large aviary, but offspring have been successfully raised in flight cages and even in large, regular cages.

Pair Formation: The male and the female have to be introduced to each other very gradually, or the process of getting acquainted may come to a quick and tragic end because the weaker bird is killed. If the birds are kept in cages, they should have only visual contact across the bars for several days. They may be combined in the same quarters only when the cock's aggressive behavior changes to courtship display. If you keep your birds in aviaries, the female should move into the breeding aviary several days before the male; this way she feels comfortable and secure before the male appears. Dense, low vegetation or loose piles of twigs offer her additional cover and safety. Even in this situation it is still helpful if the two birds can first get to know each other across bars (house them in adjacent aviaries temporarily or keep the male in a cage inside the female's aviary for a few days). During the courtship display the cock dances around the hen on the ground, follows her wherever she flies, and sings to her. The impressive black tail and the contrasting white tail coverts serve as optical stimu-

Descriptions of Popular Softbills

lants. The courtship lasts for about 1 week.

Nest: The female builds the nest without help from the male. She prefers a half-open or completely enclosed nesting box. (You can use semi-enclosed boxes or nest boxes designed for parrots; enlarge the entry hole if necessary.) For constructing the base of the nest you can supply plant fibers, small roots, wood shavings, leaves, animal hair, and similar items. For lining the nest, shamas like to use coconut fibers. It takes a bird about 3 days to build a nest. The female usually does all the sitting on the eggs, but both parents are involved in the rearing of the young.

Note: It sometimes happens that the male pursues the brooding female or destroys the eggs. If that is the case, he must be removed from the aviary until the nestlings have hatched.

Rearing the young: Once the young have hatched, the male parent usually takes part in feeding them without harming them. Once the fledglings can fend for themselves they must be moved out of the breeding aviary. The males in particular should be housed in separate cages or serious fighting may break out among the siblings.

Singing lessons: Juvenile shamas learn to sing primarily from their male parent. This is why you should house the young cocks where they can hear him. Tapes of shamas singing and the song of wild birds outdoors are also helpful.

Breeding Data

Nesting sites in nature: Preferably holes in big bamboo stalks and other trees, usually no higher than 6 feet from the ground and sometimes just above the ground.

Incubation and nestling care: The female builds the nest and sits on the eggs without help from the male, but both parents feed the nestlings.

Clutch: Four to five eggs (more rarely three or six). The eggs are a pale bluish green and with brownish spots. Size: 12 × 17.2 mm.

Incubation period: 11 days.

Nestling period: 12 to 13 days.

Related Species

Dayal

(Also called dayal thrush. Dayal may be spelled dyal or dhyal. Sometimes called magpie robin; see note under shama on page 71.)

Copsychus saularis (Linné, 1768)

Photo on page 46

Distribution: This bird is found in many subspecies over large parts of Southeast Asia, including India, Indochina, Sri Lanka, the Andaman Islands, southern China, and many islands of the Malay Archipelago. *Habitat:* Open forests, bushy landscapes, and mangrove thickets; also gardens and parks in cities. *Overall length:* 8 inches (20 cm). *Appearance and disposition:* Somewhat stouter than the shama and with a shorter tail. The plumage of the male and female differs: the black on the tail is more grayish in the female. Dayals forage for food primarily on and near the ground, but they also drink nectar. *Requirements in captivity:* Essentially the same as for the shama. *Voice:* This bird's song, too, is loud, melodic, and varied.

Snowy-headed Robin Chat

Cossypha niveicapilla (Lafresnaye, 1838)

Distribution: Central Africa south of the Sahara from Senegal to southwestern Ethiopia. *Habitat:* Wooded areas with dense lower growth as well as dry savannahs and parks. *Overall length:* 8 inches (20 cm). *Appearance and disposition:* The sexes are hard to tell apart, although the females are generally somewhat smaller than the males. The snowy-headed robin chats live in pairs, are strictly territorial, and usually stay close to the ground. They feed primarily on insects and only rarely on berries. *Requirements in captivity:* These birds are more demanding than shamas, dayals, or dama thrushes and should therefore be kept only by bird fanciers with extensive experience in handling softbills. They are not suited to life in a cage and should have either an indoor aviary at least 6 feet long or, preferably, a well-planted outdoor aviary. If they have an outdoor aviary, the birds can spend the summer there, starting around the end of April and moving back indoors in the fall. *Food:* Commercial insect food for thrushlike birds supplemented by lots of live insects (mealworms, crickets, maggots, or wax moth larvae). Some individuals also eat chopped apple. For raising young they must have live insects. Snowy-headed robin chats should live in pairs; don't combine more than two birds because they are very aggressive. *Breeding:* These birds breed in half-open cavities and therefore prefer semienclosed nest boxes or niches as nest supports. Move the male out of the aviary once the eggs are laid because he is likely to attack the brooding female and may even go after the young birds. Generally the male takes no part in the rearing of the young anyhow. *Voice:* This species produces excellent singers with a great talent for mimicking.

Dama Thrush

Geokichla citrina (Latham, 1790)
Photo on page 46

Distribution: This bird occurs in many subspecies throughout much of southern Asia, including India, the Himalayas, southern China, Bangladesh, Burma, Thailand, Malaysia, Indochina, and a number of islands in Southeast Asia. *Habitat:* Dense woods and gardens that offer plenty of cover. *Overall length:* 8¼ inches (21 cm). *Appearance and disposition:* Typical, stout thrush shape. The back of the male is bluish gray, that of the female more brownish. These shy birds live singly or in pairs mostly close to the ground. *Requirements in captivity:* Basically the same as for shamas. Dama thrushes remain timid for quite a long time in captivity, however, and are more comfortable in a thickly planted aviary than in a cage. They are not at all aggressive and are therefore good candidates for a community aviary. They eat commercial insect food and are grateful for variety in the form of live insects, worms, small snails, and occasionally berries. *Voice:* This bird's song is very pleasing and reminiscent of that of the European song thrush (*Turdus philomenus*).

Rufous-bellied Niltava

Niltava sundara (Hodgson, 1837)
Photo on page 45

Distribution: The Himalayan region from Pakistan to southwestern China, Burma, and northwestern Thailand. *Habitat:* Mountain forests with good ground cover and underbrush, usually near water and as high as 8000 feet (2500 m). *Overall length:* 6¼ to 6½ inches (16-16.5 cm). *Appearance and disposition:* Females are easy to distinguish from the conspicuously colored males by their much more subdued brownish plumage with a characteristic blue spot on the throat and a white band between the throat and the breast. The rufous-bellied niltava resembles the European robin (*Erithacus rubecula*) in its habits, spending much of its time close to the ground. The nests are usually built in rock niches or in tree holes. *Feeding:* These birds live mostly on insects, which are collected on the ground or caught in the air in typical flycatcher fashion; during the winter when not many insects are around, berries form a larger part of the diet. *Requirements in captivity:* Rufous-bellied niltavas are recommended only for experienced bird keepers. They should preferably be housed in an aviary with plants and given a diet consisting mostly of soft insect food with lots of live insects. They also should get berries (red or black elderberries or chopped raisins, for example). Very few of these birds have so far reproduced in captivity, but if they do attempt to breed, they should be given a semi-enclosed nesting box. *Voice:* Rufous-bellied niltavas have extremely pleasant voice. Like the mockingbird of the southern regions of the United States, they are excellent mimies. Frequently they can be heard incorporating fragments of other bird songs into their songs.

Description of Popular Softbills

The Zosteropidae Family (White-eyes)

White-eyes are gregarious birds. The family consists of many species found in Africa, across southern Asia, in Australia, and on islands near these areas. The genus *Zosterops* includes over 60 species and is the largest in the family. In fact, it is one of the largest genera in the entire bird world. All the members of the Zosteropidae family are very similar in both appearance and behavior. A ring around the eyes made up of tiny, usually white feathers is characteristic of all of them, with minor variations in different species. In some, the ring is broken near the cere, and in the black-ringed zosterop it is black.

During the reproductive cycle, white-eyes eat mostly insects; the rest of the time their diet consists largely of fruits, berries, and nectar. When feeding on fruit, they have a peculiar habit of enlarging small holes or cracks by poking in the beak and then opening it wide. In some species the eggs hatch after only 10 days plus a few hours, setting a record not only within their own family but among all birds. When not engaged in producing and rearing young, white-eyes often live in flocks together with other kinds of birds. Some white-eyes are migratory, traveling impressive distances twice a year. Chestnut-flanked white-eyes, for instance, make a round-trip journey of 4000 miles (7000 km) or more every year.

White-eyes are lively birds and make charming companions. The species most popular among bird fanciers are the Indian, the Japanese, and the chestnut-flanked white-eyes.

Indian White-eye

(Also known as Oriental white-eye.)
Zosterops palpebrosus (Temminck, 1824)
Photos on inside front cover and on back cover
Drawings on pages 22, 26, 34, 49, 50, 51, and 66

Distribution: Southeastern Afghanistan, India, Indochina, southwestern China, the Laccadive Islands, Sri Lanka, the Andaman Islands, and the Sunda Islands. There are many subspecies that can be divided into three main groups. One group has gray underparts; the other two have yellow underparts. *Habitat:* Woods, bushy vegetation, mangrove thickets, plantations, gardens; in the Himalayas, Indian white-eyes are found up to 7500 feet (2300 m). *Overall length:* 4 inches (10 cm). *Appearance:* Some subspecies have gray underparts, others have a yellow stripe running down the middle. The eye ring has a small break near the beak. The two sexes are very similar in coloring, with the male displaying a somewhat brighter yellow at the throat and undertail coverts. *Behavior:* These birds are arboreal and are seen on the ground only rarely. They are very gregarious, living in groups outside the mating season and roaming in search of trees that are in flower or bearing fruit. Indian white-eyes live primarily on berries, nectar, and insects. When they find larger fruit, they peck a hole into it and drink its juice. *Voice:* Indian white-eyes maintain very active vocal contact with each other through call notes and alarm calls. The males also sing softly and, during the mating season, utter surprisingly loud cries.

Requirements in Captivity

These cheerful birds lead an active communal life and become tame quickly. They have no diffi-

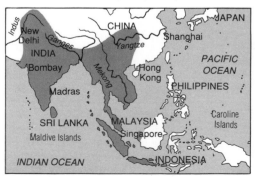

cult demands for housing or food and sometimes live quite long; 10 years is not exceptional (see page 67).

Housing: White-eyes are quite diminutive, but they are used to much activity and need as large a cage as you can manage.

Cage: A wire cage is better than a box or a glass cage because it offers more opportunity for climbing. Branches used as perches must be easy to exchange since they get sticky in no time from the fruit and nectar the birds feed on. Food cups and baths should be in the upper part of the cage because white-eyes get on the floor only reluctantly (in a cage you can mount them on the grating or put them in the bathhouse; in an aviary, place them on the food stand). The feet of white-eyes are adapted to climbing and are not very efficient for moving on the ground. When flying freely in a room, the birds enjoy getting wet among leafy plants that have been watered with a spray bottle.

Indoor aviary: An aviary obviously allows your Indian white-eyes greater freedom of movement; it should be set up along the same lines as a cage.

Outdoor aviary: As denizens of higher, mountainous regions in nature, Indian white-eyes can — after they have become well acclimated — spend much of the year outdoors. They can stay out even in the winter as long as the proper precautions are taken (see page 26). My own Indian white-eyes like to be out on the balcony even when it snows and the temperature is below freezing, and they have to be forcefully persuaded to return indoors in the evening.

Note: Indian white-eyes are found from the Himalayas to the Sunda Islands, and there may well be some subspecies that don't thrive in the cold. Caution and close observation are therefore in order.

Feeding: The recommended diet for Indian white-eyes is commercial insect food for delicate feeders (honey based). In addition to this they should always get some nectar substitute. With their long, brushlike tongues, they can drink from a tube designed for hummingbirds. A daily portion of fruit is also essential. White-eyes have a preference for soft, sweet fruits, like grapes, ripe pears, and tangerines, and they also like to gobble up cactus figs. Among live insects, soft, small arthropods are most appropriate, such as lesser mealworms, freshly hatched or very young mealworms, ant pupae, fruit flies, and enchytrids. A fresh, leafy branch infested with aphids is a welcome treat, on which the birds immediately and excitedly get to work, hunting for the insects.

Note: In white-eyes that don't get enough exercise or whose diet is not rich enough in carotene, the colors of the plumage can fade. Green parts turn gray, and the bright yellow on the throat and the undertail coverts becomes diluted. If this happens, it's time to review the birds' diet and living conditions (see page 63).

Disposition: Indian white-eyes are dependent on each other's company and should be kept in groups of two or more. In a pair, the two partners spend much of their time nestled together and gently combing through each other's feathers. There is no problem in combining them with other kinds of birds, such as exotic finches, and they can hold their own even against larger birds. White-eyes have such a strong need for contact that a single bird quickly joins other, unrelated birds of similarly social nature. Also, even if there are several white-eyes in an aviary, a single white-eye left when the others have paired will seek the company of other species. If your birds live in cages, don't keep more than one pair per cage. If there is room enough, add another type of bird (such as an exotic finch) rather than more white-eyes. A flock of white-eyes should live together only in a large, well-planted aviary. Only under these conditions can they display the full range of behavior they are capable of.

Despite their affection for each other, white-eyes are quite belligerent. A conflict can break out for no obvious reason, with the birds going after each other, furiously snapping their beaks. If there is enough room for them to get away from each other and hide, the two fighters are soon seen huddled closely together and pecking each other's plumage. Specialists in animal behavior interpret the intensive mutual preening of white-eyes as a soothing gesture necessary for birds with a high degree of intraspecies aggressivity.

Voice: Indian white-eyes are almost constantly uttering some of their many contact calls, usually composed of one or two syllables. The male's modest song is pleasant to the ear. He likes to sing from a well-hidden spot (in the foliage of a plant, for instance), and his song is reminiscent of the aquatic warbler (*Acrocephalus palustris*) or the icterine warbler (*Hippolais icterina*). Unmated males are especially diligent singers.

Breeding

Indian white-eyes have been successfully bred in outdoor and indoor aviaries as well as in cages. Because the sexes look so much alike, however, it takes some luck to end up with a true pair when you buy two birds. If you buy four birds, the chances are better. You will have to remove the two extra birds when a pair has formed and starts its reproductive cycle; otherwise there will be constant and violent fighting, which could not only ruin the breeding attempt but also end in the death of one of the birds. Some breeding pairs even attack birds belonging to other species with green plumage.

Nest: The cock and the hen work together building the nest. In nature they make cup-shaped nests in the crotch of a branch. First they wind a bunch of plant wool or similar material around the branches, and into this they fit a small cup made of grass stalks and plant fibers. Your broody white-eyes need bushes, evergreens, or sturdy vines (Boston ivy or climbing false buckwheat) to build their nests on. They can construct a base from cotton wool, and then you should give them coconut fibers, grass stalks, or similar plant material for assembling the cup. Many birds also accept man-made nest supports (see page 48).

Incubation: The two parents frequently relieve each other in sitting on the eggs, and sometimes they both sit on the nest at the same time. Once I was able to observe a unique form of parental care. My Indian white-eyes had built their nest just where the roof covering part of the aviary ended. Now, whenever it rained, the male stood on the rim of the nest and spread his wings to keep the nest and the brooding hen from getting wet.

Rearing the Young: The only rearing food these birds consider for their young is live food, especially aphids, mealworms (freshly hatched or very young ones), blue bottlefly and lesser mealworm larvae, fruit flies, and other small, soft insects. Frozen ant pupae and frozen young crickets are only rarely accepted, and the parents don't offer fruit to the nestlings until they have learned to fly (see drawing on page 51).

The areas around the eyes and the throat are naked when the young birds leave the nest. The eye ring doesn't grow in until 5 or 6 days later when the youngsters have developed their full flying powers. Apparently this is a kind of grace period during which other, strange members of the species refrain from attacking them. Indian white-eyes leave the juveniles in peace while they lack the eye ring and they move awkwardly among the bushes. The parent birds coexist peacefully with their offspring much longer and sometimes go on feeding them even after starting a new brood.

Rearing Young Where the Parents Can Fly Free: Indian white-eyes are excellent candidates for raising their young outdoors where the parent birds can fly unrestricted (see page 51). They find their way around a garden quickly and are so inconspicuous that they run little danger of being caught. I tried this method with my white-eyes for the first time in 1986. The parents provided so well for their

Bulbuls.
Above, left: Red-eared bulbul (*Pycnonotus jocosus*).
Above, right: Red-vented bulbul (tonki or kala bulbul) (*P. cafer*). Below, left: White-eared bulbul (*P. leucogenys*). Below, right: Gray bulbul (*P. capensis*).

young under these conditions that the two older fledglings left the nest after only 11 days and the youngest one after only 10. The parents fed the nestlings not only insects they caught but also generous amounts of mealworms, fruit flies, and blue bottlefly larvae I made available to them.

Breeding Data

Nesting sites in nature: In the forks of thickly leafed branches; nests are built 3 to 20 feet (1–6 m) above ground; they are loosely woven of grass, moss, cobwebs, and plant wool.
Incubation and nestling care: The partners take turns sitting on the nest.
Clutch: Two to four (usually three) eggs; the eggs are solid colored, a delicate bluish green; egg size: 15.2 × 11.5 mm.
Incubation period: 10 to 11 days.
Nestling period: 10 to 13 days.

Related Species

Japanese White-eye

Zosterops japonicus (Temminck and Schlegel, 1847)

Distribution: Japanese white-eyes are distributed widely in the Far East: from Japan across the Ryukyu Islands to Taiwan and Hainan, and on large parts of mainland China, namely from Shensi, Honan, and Shantung in the north to Indochina in the south. The subspecies found on the mainland is often called the Chinese white-eye. *Habitat:* Plantations, gardens, light woods. *Overall length:* 4¼ inches (11 cm). *Appearance and disposition:* Simi-

lar to the Indian white-eye, but the flanks are brownish to reddish yellow in many races. *Requirements in captivity:* The same as for Indian white-eyes. *Voice:* Similar to that of Indian White-eyes.

Chestnut-flanked White-eye

Zosterops erythropleurus (Swinhoe, 1863)
Photo on page 18

Distribution: Along the Ussuri and Amur Rivers on the Russo-Chinese border, and parts of eastern Manchuria. This is the northernmost region inhabited by any white-eyes. Chestnut-flanked white-eyes winter in Szechwan, Yunnan, eastern Burma, northern Thailand, and Vietnam. *Habitat:* Willow thickets in the taiga. Overall length: 4¼ inches (11 cm). *Appearance and disposition:* This species differs from the two already described primarily by the striking chestnut streak on the flank; its personality resembles that of the other white-eyes. *Requirements in captivity:* Similar to those for the Indian white-eye, but this species usually doesn't become quite as tame. It is better suited for an aviary than a cage. *Voice:* The chestnut-flanked white-eye's song resembles that of its Indian cousin but is more melodic and has more variety.

The Chloropseidae Family (Leafbirds)

The eight genera of this family inhabit the jungles of Southeast Asia, from the Himalayas and southern China southward across India and Indochina to Sri Lanka, Malaysia, and the Sunda Islands. Outside the mating season, leafbirds often live together with other fruit-eating birds (such as bulbuls), searching for fruits and blossoms in treetops. Their beaks, slender and curved slightly downward, and the tongue with its brushlike tip, are adapted for extracting nectar from flowers.

All leafbirds have short, strong legs and similarly colored plumage in which green predomi-

Leafbirds.
Above, left: A male orange-bellied leafbird (*Chloropsis hardwickii*). Above, right: A female orange-bellied leafbird. Below, left: Gold-fronted leafbird (*C. aurifrons*). Below, right: Blue-winged leafbird, (*C. cochinchinensis*), subspecies: Jerdon's leafbird.

nates. In some, the sexes look alike, but in others the female lacks the characteristic black markings on the head. All leafbirds are talented singers and famous for their mimicking ability that allows them to imitate the sounds of other birds and incorporate them into their own songs. The species that are most popular with bird owners are the gold-fronted, the blue-winged, and the orange-bellied leafbird.

Gold-fronted Leafbird

Chloropsis aurifrons (Temminck, 1829)
Photo on page 80
Drawing on page 23

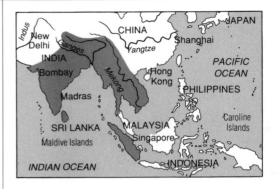

Distribution: India to southern Thailand and Indochina, Sri Lanka, and Sumatra. *Habitat:* Evergreen forests in hilly country; in the foothills of the Himalayas up to about 5800 feet (1800 m). *Overall length:* 7½ inches (19 cm). *Appearance:* No difference in plumage between the sexes (although the colors in the female may be less intense); depending on the subspecies, the throat is either blue or black with a blue, beardlike streak on the side. The gold-fronted leafbird is distinguished from the otherwise similar blue-winged leafbird by its golden forehead and green primaries. *Behavior:* Leafbirds live together in pairs or small groups that often include birds of different species. They are found near trees that bear fruit, spending most of their time in the treetops, and are only rarely seen on the ground. *Voice:* Extremely varied song that can be pleasant or raucous and includes many calls and musical motifs, some imitated from other kinds of birds, but also some shrill and rasping sounds.

Requirements in Captivity

The gold-fronted leafbird is the most commonly imported species of *Chloropsis*. Among the reasons for its popularity are its lively song, its bright colors, and its friendly disposition. If kept properly, these birds can live 10 years or more.

Housing: Because of their aggressiveness, these softbills must be kept one per cage or small aviary. Single gold-fronted leafbirds usually become very tame in captivity and are particularly diligent singers.

Cage: Leafbirds are frugivorous, and a box cage that has three solid walls is the most practical solution for them because less of the surroundings is bespattered with bits of sticky food. If you use a wire cage, cover the side and back walls with plastic. The perches get sticky quickly and must be wiped with a damp cloth and replaced frequently. Because large amounts of wet droppings are produced, the bottom should be covered with an absorbent material, such as cat litter. Since they spend their lives in treetops in nature, gold-fronted leafbirds need a lot of climbing branches, and the food dishes and bathhouse must be mounted high up (hang them on the bars of the cage or put them on the feeding platform).

Indoor aviary: In a rather large aviary with plenty of cover, gold-fronted leafbirds can be included in a community of birds, but not with others of their own species or genus.

Outdoor aviary: Gold-fronted leafbirds that are well acclimated do well in cooler climates and can spend the summer outdoors, but they need warm quarters for winter.

Feeding: Gold-fronted leafbirds live mostly on fruit (predominantly berries and the fruits of mistletoe plants) and nectar. Except during the mating season, insects do not form a major part of their diet.

Description of Popular Softbills

In addition to all kinds of fruits, your leafbird should always have some nectar drink (see page 33), which it will imbibe from a small cup or a drinking straw by means of its brushlike tongue. Your bird should also be offered a good commercial insect food (honey based), even if it hardly consumes any of it. Generally the birds like to eat live insects, although only in small portions. They are good at catching flying insects and mealworms that are tossed into the cage.

Note: Your gold-fronted leafbird is delighted whenever you give it some branches with berries on them; the berries of mountain ash and firethorn are especially appreciated.

Disposition: Gold-fronted leafbirds are quiet birds. They adjust quickly to their new surroundings, become tame and friendly, and soon will hop onto your hand to get a favorite treat. They sleep long and deeply, retiring to their sleeping places in the late afternoon and not opening their eyes again until 7 or 8 the next morning. They are such sound sleepers that you can hardly rouse them even when you reach into their cage. Leafbirds like to take frequent and unhurried baths. Give them an opportunity during their daily free-flying session to bathe among leafy indoor plants that you have watered with a spray bottle.

Voice: The highly varied song of the gold-fronted leafbird is considered one of the finest of all bird songs. It contains a wealth of motifs and musical calls but also some less pleasant shrill and rasping notes. The gold-fronted leafbird is an accomplished mimic, incorporating the calls and songs of other birds — sometimes reproduced with astonishing fidelity — into its own song. It never stops learning and keeps adding to its repertoire. The cheerful singing of a gold-fronted leafbird is not for everybody, however. Every so often you find a bird in whose song the unpleasant notes predominate. Presumably these are cocks that had not finished training their voices when they were caught, or females. The latter sing, too, but not as much and with less variety.

Note: You can enhance your bird's song as described in connection with shamas (see pages 24 and 71) by playing tapes of model bird songs for your leafbird to listen to. If you have access to a good singer, try to make arrangements to tape him. Tapes of bird songs may also be available in pet shops.

Breeding

Breeding gold-fronted leafbirds is extremely difficult and has been accomplished only rarely so far. The first breeding success in Germany came in 1979, when a bird fancier who had been trying to get offspring from his gold-fronted leafbirds for 25 years finally succeeded. The main problems are
• the difficulty of accurately sexing the birds; cocks and hens are outwardly indistinguishable
• the belligerent attitude of the birds toward each other; the cock will repeatedly and violently attack the female even while the two birds are raising a brood together

Breeding Quarters: The birds need a well-planted aviary. Dense vegetation on the ground (ferns) is especially important so that the hen can dive into it and hide when the cock pursues her ferociously.

Nest: Leafbirds build free-standing nests on forked branches. They need long hemp and coconut fibers and sisal to build with.

Rearing the Young: The rearing food should consist entirely of live or freshly killed insects, particularly of medium-sized crickets and frozen ant pupae. The bird fancier mentioned earlier reports that the parent birds induced the nestlings to open their gapes by singing a short, not very loud song as they approached the nest with food. The young birds stayed together with their parents for a long time and still screamed for their parents when they were separated from them at the age of three months. After the reproductive cycle was completed, things quieted down considerably. In this relatively peaceful atmosphere the parents no longer fought and the couple could be wintered over together.

Description of Popular Softbills

Related Species

Orange-bellied Leafbird

(Also known as Hardwick's leafbird and bluebearded leafbird.)
Chloropsis hardwickei (Jardine and Selby, 1830)
Photo on page 80

Distribution: From the Himalayas and hilly sections of eastern Pakistan to southern China, northwestern Thailand, parts of Assam and Laos, Tonkin, and Malaysia. This species is found at altitudes of 7800 feet (2400 m) and more in the mountains, which is higher than any other leafbird ventures. *Habitat:* Open mountain woods. *Overall length:* 8 inches (20 cm). *Appearance and disposition:* The orange-bellied leafbird differs from the other species of its genus by having a much more extensive black mask (it reaches down to the breast) and a yellowish orange abdomen. The female lacks the black mask and the deep blue parts on the wings and tail. These sexual differences in plumage are much more obvious than those of any other leafbirds of this genus. Orange-bellied leafbirds are similar in behavior to their gold-fronted cousins but are extremely aggressive and often not as friendly toward people. *Requirements in captivity:* The same as for gold-fronted leafbirds. *Voice:* These birds are excellent singers and mimics; their song is mellifluous and steady but also quite loud. *Name:* The name blue-bearded leafbird, which is sometimes applied to the orange-bellied leafbird, is also used for the tiny lesser green or blue-whiskered leafbird (*Chloropsis cyanopogon*), which measures only 5½ inches (14 cm).

Blue-winged Leafbird

(Also known as yellow-headed leafbird; a western subspecies goes by the name of Jerdon's leafbird.)
Chloropsis cochinchinensis (Gmelin, 1788)
Photo on page 80

Distribution: Large parts of India; Bangladesh, Assam, and Indochina; from southwestern China to the Sunda Islands and Sri Lanka. *Habitat:* Woods and the edges of woods, preferably in hilly country. *Overall length:* 7 inches (18 cm). *Appearance and disposition:* This bird looks very much like the gold-fronted leafbird but lacks the golden forehead, having merely a pale yellow rim around the somewhat smaller black mask; in some subspecies the entire upper part of the head is yellow. The primaries are bright blue, as are the outer tail feathers. The female does not have a black mask. *Requirements in captivity:* The same as for the gold-fronted leafbird. *Voice:* This leafbird is a remarkable mimic and persistent singer.

Pycnonotidae Family (Bulbuls)

The bulbuls are a quite uniform family of passerines about the size of starlings or thrushes. Because of their soft plumage and their elongated, hairlike crests that often stick up like fancy hairdos, they are sometimes called hair birds. The family is made up of about 30 genera that include approximately 120 species. Bulbuls are indigenous to tropical and subtropical Asia and to Africa. Some species range as far as the Mediterranian regions of Africa and Asia Minor. The original habitat of bulbuls consisted of dense forests, jungles, areas with some trees and bushes, and — in Africa — oases and savannahs with scattered trees. Now these birds have in many places learned to live close to humans.

Description of Popular Softbills

Outside the mating season bulbuls live in small groups that often include several species of bulbuls as well as other birds. They are almost exclusively frugivorous, with insects playing a negligible part in their diet except during rearing time.

Most bulbuls produce melodious call notes but no real song. There is one exception, however: the yellow-headed bulbul of Malaysia and the Greater Sunda Islands, which is considered one of the best songbirds of the world.

Red-eared Bulbul

Pycnonotus jocosus (Linné, 1758)
Photos on page 79 and on back cover
Drawings on pages 14, 47, and 63

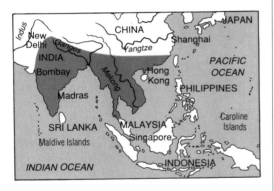

Distribution: The Indian subcontinent except for Pakistan; southern China, Indochina, and northern Malaysia; also introduced to Mauritius, parts of Australia, and Florida. *Habitat:* The edges of jungles and open landscapes with some trees (for instance, parks, plantations, and gardens). *Overall length:* 8 inches (20 cm). *Appearance:* Males and females have similar plumage. Juveniles are more brownish on the upper parts and have a brownish black head without the red ear patch of the adults; the adult plumage grows in between weeks 8 and 10. *Behavior:* The birds avoid dense forests and often live near human settlements, sometimes even building their nests on vine-covered verandas and walls. Red-eared bulbuls are very spirited birds and highly expressive in behavior. *Voice:* This species utters melodious and often loud call notes (contact calls, alarm calls, and calls to attract other birds) that are sometimes reminiscent of those of orioles. The song of the male consists of a soft, steady chattering.

Requirements in Captivity

The stately red-eared bulbuls win our admiration because of their attractive appearance and their spirited nature. They are very social and should always be kept in pairs. They can — at least when not involved in the reproductive cycle — be combined with other birds of similar size. Never keep a pair together with other bulbuls, however. This applies to all species. If you do, major conflicts inevitably erupt that may end in fatalities. Newly purchased birds are very nervous and timid, requiring a great deal of patience and empathy on the part of the owner. This species is therefore better for someone with some experience in caring for wild birds. If kept properly, red-eared bulbuls often live quite long in captivity (over 10 years).

Housing: Because of their size and stormy ways, red-eared bulbuls should have plenty of room. The larger the cage, the better.

Cage: Because they startle easily, bulbuls are better off in a box cage (see page 13) than in a wire cage that is open on all sides. Glass cages are not desirable because the birds find it hard to get used to the glass. A layer of cat litter on the bottom is recommended because bulbuls — who consume a lot of fruit — produce voluminous, soft, wet droppings. Don't line the cage bottom with newspapers, or soaked pieces of it will be kicked all over the cage.

Indoor aviary: An indoor aviary is preferable to a cage because it makes more allowance for the birds' temperamental disposition (for setting up the aviary, see page 14).

Outdoor aviary: There is no need for dense

Description of Popular Softbills

vegetation since these birds don't seek cover but spend most of their time noisily moving about in the upper third of the aviary. Red-eared bulbuls are hardy and can, after proper acclimation, withstand low temperatures, so that they can spend the best part of the year outdoors. If they have access to a lightly heated shelter where it stays above freezing, they can stay outside all year (see page 26).

Feeding: Red-eared bulbuls are unproblematic, omnivorous eaters that like a lot of fruit and berries. Fresh figs are a special treat, since figs make up a major part of their diet in nature. Sweet grapes and raisins are also welcome. In addition to fruit, you should give them insect food every day, such as the honey food described on page 34. Red-eared bulbuls have no great fondness for live larvae and worms, but they do like flying insects, which they are good at catching. Bulbuls always show interest in a daily ration of nectar drink.

Note: My bulbuls don't seem very fond of commercial insect food but do enjoy mynah pellets and chick pellets. Sometimes they gobble up softened dog food, which at other times they ignore for weeks.

Disposition: Red-eared bulbuls are lively birds, but they cannot engage in their full range of behavior unless they are allowed to live in pairs. A variety of expressions accompanies everything they do. The pointed crest, which can be raised high or flattened at will, is like a barometer of moods, and body posture as well as the use of wings is an integral part of ritualized communication even outside courtship display. Two birds that have formed a bond are very loving, spending much time nestled closely together, accompanying each other on flights through the aviary or room, and always maintaining at least vocal contact.

Voice: Many and sometimes quite piercing calls are uttered during all the red-eared bulbul's activities, ranging from greetings to calling the mate to territorial defense. There are also shrill alarm and fright calls. If you have noise-sensitive neighbors, bulbuls may not be the best birds for you. The song of the male is modest and quite soft.

Breeding

Red-eared bulbuls have been bred quite often in captivity. Success is most likely in a large aviary where there is enough room for the stormy courtship displays.

Pair Formation: One of the main difficulties when breeding red-eared bulbuls is to get a true pair. Males and females are much alike in both appearance and behavior. Two birds of the same sex may act just like a heterosexual pair, build a nest and — if they are females — lay eggs and sit on them, hoping in vain for them to hatch. If you have a choice among a number of birds when you buy them, try picking the two that differ the most in coloration. This offers no guarantees (the difference can be due to age or race), but it improves your chances of ending up with a true pair.

Nest: Red-eared bulbuls are not particular about where they build their nest. If the vegetation in the aviary offers no suitable sites (such as forked branches), you can facilitate the building of a nest by providing artificial nest supports. The nest itself is open and cup-shaped. The birds use coconut fibers, sisal, and small strips of cloth, as well as bits of paper, stalks of grass, and leaves as building materials. Most building is done by the female.

Incubation: The cock and the hen take turns sitting on the eggs. Be especially considerate of the birds at this time. Usually they leave the nest anxiously when the caretaker enters the aviary but return to it quickly when he or she has left. There have been cases, however, of red-eared bulbuls kicking the eggs out of the nest after an interruption.

Rearing the Young: During the first half of the nestling period, the parents feed the nestlings live insects only; after that, fruit is accepted.

Note: Red-eared bulbuls are one kind of bird you should not let out of the aviary to forage for rearing food. They look so striking that someone might try to catch them, thinking they are escaped cage birds.

Description of Popular Softbills

Breeding Data

Nesting sites in nature: Extremely variable.
Incubation and nestling care: Both birds take turns incubating the eggs. They usually start sitting on the nest after the first egg is laid, although at first only intermittently.
Clutch: Two to three eggs; the eggs are whitish to pink, sprinkled with dark red to purple dots.
Size: 24.4 × 16.1 mm.
Incubation period: 12 to 14 days.
Nestling period: 13 to 14 days.

Related Species

White-eared Bulbul

Pycnonotus leucogenys (Gray, 1835)
Photo on page 79

Distribution: From the western coast of the Persian Gulf and Iraq to Pakistan, northwestern India, and parts of Afghanistan; also in the Himalayas and eastward to Assam. *Habitat:* Very varied; in the Himalayan regions these birds are found as high as 7800 feet (2400 m). They often live in close proximity to people. *Overall length:* 8 inches (20 cm). *Appearance and disposition:* The western subspecies have only a suggestion of a crest, whereas in some eastern subspecies the crest may extend to the beak. In behavior these birds resemble their red-eared cousins. *Requirements in captivity:* The same as for red-eared bulbuls. White-eared bulbuls often get quite tame and can live to a great age in captivity. *Voice:* Melodious call notes.

Red-vented Bulbul

(Also called tonki bulbul)
Pycnonotus cafer (Linné, 1766)
Photo on page 79

Distribution: Southeast Asia from India to southern China and Malaysia; also on Java. The red-vented bulbul has also been introduced in other places, for example on Sumatra, the Fiji Islands, and New Zealand. There are two groups of subspecies, one that occupies the eastern, and the other the western range of distribution; where the two overlap they often cross-breed. *Habitat:* Secondary forests, scrub brush, gardens, open woods. *Overall length:* 7 to 8 inches (18–20 cm) (eastern subspecies); 8 to 8¾ inches (20–22 cm) (western subspecies). *Appearance and disposition:* Western subspecies: The plumage is mostly blackish, the ear coverts, brown, the undertail coverts, red. The eastern subspecies are lighter, with the throat, ear coverts, and underparts a dirty white and the undertail coverts, yellow. In behavior these birds resemble the red-eared bulbuls. *Requirements:* The same as for red-eared bulbuls. Birds of the western subspecies are often very aggressive, and pairs should therefore be housed individually. *Voice:* Melodious song.

Gray Bulbul

Pycnonotus capensis (Linné, 1766)
Photo on page 79

Distribution: From southeastern Turkey to South Africa. There are seven groups of subspecies, among them the masked, cape, and gray bulbuls. *Habitat:* Palm groves, wadis with scattered bushes, as well as towns, gardens, and fruit plantations. *Overall length:* 7 to 8 inches (18–20 cm). *Appearance and disposition:* Overall appearance: dark brownish gray. Head and throat: black. Resembles the red-eared bulbul in behavior. *Requirements:* Similar to those of the red-eared bulbul. *Voice:* A loud, flutelike song made up of short strophes.

The Sturnidae Family (Starlings)

Starlings were originally birds of the Old World, inhabiting primarily Africa and Southeast Asia. Today they are found all over the world because some species were introduced to other parts of the earth. The European starling, for instance, has

Description of Popular Softbills

spread to North America, South Africa, and New Zealand; the Indian mynah (*Acridotheres tristis*) has found its way from Southeast Asia to Australia and South Africa; and the crested mynah (*A. cristatellus*) from Indochina has even been brought to British Columbia (Canada). The Sturnidae family includes 42 genera with 115 species.

Some members of the starling family sport bright colors, but most of them are dark colored, some with an iridescent sheen. Many walk on the ground with a deliberate or waddling gait. Starlings are generally gregarious and quite often breed in colonies. Most of them build their nests in holes. A large part of their diet is made up of fruit, although the Sturnidae are basically omnivorous. At harvest time they travel in huge flocks and often do extensive crop damage in orchards and vineyards. During their breeding time, however, they devour many insect pests.

Starlings have a large range of vocal utterances. They make whistling, clicking, and rasping sounds, and many also imitate voices and other sounds.

A number of birds belonging to the Sturnidae family can be kept in captivity, but — if only because of their size — they should be housed in an aviary. All of them have similar demands. Since they are so gregarious, several birds can be kept together, either all of the same species or together with other birds of similar size.

Mynah
Gracula religiosa (Linné, 1758)
Photos on page 17 and on back cover
Drawings on page 9 and 63

Distribution: Parts of eastern India, in the Himalayan regions from Kumaon to southern China, and from Indochina to Malaysia, as well as many Southeast Asian islands. Mynahs have also been introduced on Christmas Island and on Oahu (Hawaii). There are several subspecies, including the greater India hill mynah (*G. r. intermedia*) and the Java hill mynah (*G. r. religiosa*). *Habitat:* Treetops on the

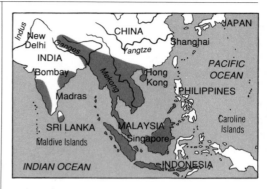

edge of dense forests or near clearings; often fig trees bearing fruit and sometimes berry bushes; rarely on the ground. *Overall length:* About 12 inches (30 cm) (India hill mynah); 12 to 14 inches (30–35 cm) (Java hill mynah). *Appearance:* In the India hill mynah, the skin patches below the eyes and on the nape are connected, which they are not in the Java hill mynah. The sexes look alike. The plumage of juvenile birds is duller before the first molt and does not have the metallic gloss of the adults. *Behavior:* Outside the breeding season, mynahs live in small bands of five to six birds or sometimes in huge flocks made up of a hundred or more birds (including other large fruit eaters) that descend on fig trees with ripe fruit. Mynahs live mainly on fruits and berries, especially wild figs, but also on nectar and insects, catching termites in the air. They sleep singly or in pairs on branches with thick foliage or in tree holes. The pair bond lasts for life.

Requirements in Captivity
As mimics, mynahs are second to no other birds, including parrots. They are extremely gregarious but not very neat roommates. They eat voluminously and produce equally voluminous amounts of soft, smelly droppings. They need the constant company of others of their kind or, as a substitute, the attention of human companions. People who are out working during the day should not buy a mynah.

Description of Popular Softbills

Housing: When you plan where your mynah will live, you'll have to keep in mind the bird's size and need for exercise.

Cage: Since the table manners of a mynah leave something to be desired — pieces of food can be flung far — a box cage (see page 13) makes sense. If you use a wire cage or an indoor aviary, you will want to line the side walls with plastic or cover the wall behind the aviary or cage with washable wall paper. A cage should be at least 32 inches (80 cm) long so that the bird has enough room to hop around in it. The bars of a mynah cage have to be sturdier than those for smaller birds and spaced farther apart, but they should not be far enough apart to let the bird get its head caught between them.

Accessories: Food and water dishes must be securely mounted to keep the strong birds from tossing them around. Dishes designed for parrots, which can be hung on the cage wires, work well. They should be located within easy reach of a perch but where they are safe from droppings. The perches should be thick enough that the birds' claws can't quite reach around them. Just as for other birds, natural branches are easier on the feet than hardwood dowels. Use only very few branches so they won't cut down the open space for hopping. Probably there won't be room enough inside the cage for a really twiggy branch, but you can make up for this by setting up a climbing tree near the cage for the bird to play in when it is flying freely in the room. It is essential that a cage for a mynah have a clean-out drawer because the masses of wet excreta make it necessary to change the bottom covering every day. Newspaper has the advantage of not costing anything. Cat litter is much more absorbent but is dusty. It should be used only if there is a grate separating the bottom tray from the rest of the cage.

Indoor aviary: If you don't have a lot of time to devote to your mynah you should house it in an indoor aviary. There it can at least fly a little and find things to do to fill up time. The same rules apply to setting up an indoor aviary as for a cage.

Outdoor aviary: In the summer, mynahs can be kept in an outdoor aviary, on a balcony or terrace, or in the garden. Living outdoors fits well with their natural enjoyment of movement. If you plan an outdoor aviary you may want to consider keeping more than one mynah. These birds are friendly toward their keepers even if kept as pairs, although pairs are not quite as tame as single birds.

Bathing: Mynahs love to take baths but are quite messy about it (see drawing on page 9). When you let your mynah fly freely, pour some water into an earthenware flower pot saucer (approximately 8 inches [20 cm] in diameter) and place it on the floor, but not too close to any furniture if you don't want it to get splashed. If your mynah is hand tame, you should teach it to bathe in the sink where, standing in water up to its belly, it can splash to its heart's content.

Sleeping place: Many mynahs like to sleep in an enclosed cavity, and you can oblige your bird by building it a sleeping box [dimensions: 8 × 8 × 8 inches (20 × 20 × 20 cm)]. Make sure the entry hole is large enough. The sleeping box should be mounted outside the cage because space inside a cage is so limited. In an aviary this is not necessary.

Feeding: Mynahs are omnivorous, stilling their hunger mostly with fruit and berries. They also need protein from animal sources (mealworms and other insects), however. Other good sources of proteins are cottage cheese, lean beef, dog food, and bird food mixtures for softbills. There is a special mynah food that comes in pellet form and has the benefit of considerably reducing the amount of droppings. A mynah should not be fed these pellets to the exclusion of everything else because the birds' digestive system is designed for food with a high water content. Still, mynah pellets do have their place as a nutritious dietary addition.

Acclimation: Most mynahs sold at pet stores are young birds that were taken from the nest in their country of origin and then hand reared. They consequently become very attached to people. Check to see whether your bird is still very young or more mature and independent. A very young bird — one that may still be begging for food — requires a great deal of attention at the beginning. Your mynah should have peace and quiet during the first few hours in its new home to help it get oriented without distractions. Since it is already familiar with humans, you can soon start talking to it and offering it treats. If it eats from your hand, you can relax. An older bird must be acclimated as described on page 22.

Disposition: Mynahs are very gregarious and want to be part of your life. They also have a great need for exercise and should never go without a daily session of free flying.

Although mynahs become quite tame, they don't like being grabbed. A tame mynah will hop onto your hand and let you gently scratch it with your finger, especially on the head, where it can't reach with its bill.

Note: Your mynah has to be tame before you can let it fly freely in a room. Even then you should keep it out of your best rooms because it can leave behind large, white droppings. You may also want to protect yourself by wearing an old overshirt or jacket.

Voice: In addition to their gift for speech and imitation, mynahs also have an impressive repertoire of whistles, calls, and many other more or less musical sounds. As in the case of parrots, the talent for speech varies from individual to individual. If you want a good talker, your best bet is to buy a young greater India hill mynah. Males and females can become equally good talkers.

Where and how a mynah is housed makes a big difference in how well the bird learns to talk. A bird that lives in a cage in the living room in close contact with the family learns more quickly than one kept in an aviary, especially if it spends a lot of time alone. Mynahs, like everyone else, must practice to become perfect, and your bird's words became steadily clearer if you repeat them over and over (preferably the same person should do all the teaching). It's easier to learn a few words at a time than many all at once. In addition to words, mynahs also imitate bird songs, whistled tunes, and all kinds of noises occurring in their surroundings.

Note: Mynahs use their voices not only frequently but also in a high decibel range. If you live in an apartment building with thin walls or keep your mynah outdoors, it may be a good idea to check how noise tolerant your neighbors are. It is best to try to avoid problems *before* they even begin to develop.

Breeding

Not many people have been successful at breeding mynahs thus far. This may be because the sexes are hard to tell apart by appearance, making it hard to obtain a true pair. Another possible reason for failure may be that hand-reared mynahs that are imprinted to humans may no longer be able to form a proper mating bond with their own kind.

Nest: Mynahs can be bred only in a large aviary. Since they like to breed in enclosed cavities, you can build a nest box for them with an entry hole of appropriate size. Commercially available nest boxes intended for pigeons or kestrels are also accepted by mynahs, as are hollowed-out tree limbs. What is important is that the top be removable so that you can reach into the nest. Thin twigs, feathers, hay, and straw are used as nesting materials.

Rearing the Young: In addition to their usual food, the birds mostly need live insects for their young. During the first few days after the nestlings have hatched, small insects should be given (freshly hatched mealworms and ant pupae); later you can add larger ones up to the size of fully grow crickets.

Breeding Data

Nesting sites in nature: In tree holes (old woodpecker holes) 30 to 45 feet (10–15 m) above ground. Sometimes several pairs breed in separate holes in the same tree.
Incubation and nestling care: Both parents collaborate in building the nest and brooding the young.
Clutch: Two to three eggs. Color: turquoise with reddish or dark brown dots. Size: 36.2 × 25.6 mm.
Incubation period: About 15 days.
Nestling period: About 28 days.

Description of Popular Softbills

Related Species

Pagoda Mynah
Temenuchus pagodarum (Gmelin, 1789)
Photos on inside back cover and back cover

Distribution: From eastern Afghanistan across Nepal and India to Sri Lanka. *Habitat:* Light forests and open, wooded landscapes, often close to human settlements. *Overall length:* 8 inches (20 cm). *Appearance and disposition:* Both sexes have similar plumage, but the crest of the female is smaller. Juveniles also have similar coloration but are darker and lack the crest. When not in breeding condition, the birds live in small bands or larger flocks, often traveling together with other frugivorous and nectarivorous birds in search of trees bearing blossoms or fruit. They spend the night in the foliage of trees together with other birds. *Requirements in captivity:* Pagoda mynahs are better suited for an aviary than a cage. After thorough acclimation these birds can spend the entire year in an outdoor aviary (for proper conditions, see page 26). *Food:* A coarse mixed food for softbills supplemented with plenty of fruit and insects, as well as nectar drink, cottage cheese, dog food, and meat. These birds should be given large, semienclosed nest boxes both for sleeping and for raising young. Pagoda mynahs have reproduced quite often in captivity, although matching pairs is difficult because of the similarity between the sexes. As rearing food, mealworms, crickets, and maggots are used. *Voice:* These birds produce rasping and whistling sounds as well as melodic songs and imitations of other birds.

Splendid Glossy Starling
Lamprotornis splendidus (Vieillot, 1822)
Photo on page 17

Distribution: Large sections of Africa, from Senegal and Uganda in the north to Angola and Zambia in the south. *Habitat:* Forests with fruit-bearing trees (such as figs). *Overall length:* 10 inches (25 cm). *Appearance and disposition:* Splendid glossy starlings are typical, very large starlings. Both sexes look alike, as do the juveniles, although their colors are duller and lack the adults' iridescent sheen. Very gregarious. *Requirements in captivity:* Similar to those for pagoda mynahs, but this bird is less hardy and needs a soft food mixture that is high in fruit. *Voice:* Crowlike calls and whistled notes.

Superb Glossy Starling
Lamprospreo superbus (Ruppell, 1845)
Photo on page 17

Distribution: Central East Africa from southeastern Sudan and southern Ethiopia to southwestern Tanzania. *Habitat:* Savannahs with thorn bushes and acacias; also near human settlements. *Overall length:* 8 inches (20 cm). *Appearance and disposition:* Both sexes look alike; juveniles are duller. *Requirements in captivity:* Similar to those for the pagoda mynahs. Superb glossy starlings reproduce quite easily in captivity. They are very aggressive during the reproductive cycle and must be kept as separate pairs at these times. *Voice:* Babbling, whistling, and chirping sounds; also imitations of other bird voices.

Indian Mynah
Acridotheres tristis (Linné, 1766)

Distribution: From Afghanistan to Malaysia and Indochina, the Himalyan region, India, Sri Lanka, and the Andaman Islands. Has also been introduced to many other parts of the world. *Habitat:* This is one of the most common birds in its areas of distribution. It is adaptable and thrives in many different kinds of environment (open spaces, cultivated areas, pastures, gardens, and towns). It has also learned to get along with humans. Outside the breeding season, the birds travel in small bands or huge flocks that sometimes include other kinds of birds. *Overall length:* 8½ inches (22 cm). *Appearance and disposition:* Head and breast are black; underparts and back, dark chestnut brown; the primaries, black with a white wing spot; the tail is brownish black above, and the undertail coverts are white. The bill, the bare skin below the eyes, and the feet are yellow. Both sexes look alike. *Requirements in captivity:* The same as for the pagoda mynah. *Voice:* Varied calls, songs and words.

Gold-crested Grackle
Ampeliceps coronatus (Blyth, 1842)

Distribution: From northeastern India and Bangladesh to Thailand and Indochina. *Habitat:* Forests, where the birds spend most of their time moving around in pairs or small bands in the tree tops. *Overall length:* 8¼ inches (21 cm). *Appearance and disposition:* The gold-crested grackle looks much like a miniature mynah but lacks the yellow wattles on the head. The plumage is basically an iridescent black; the top of the head, the ceres, and the throat are yellow; and the feathers on the forehead form a small crest. The area around the eyes is naked and a yellowish orange. The outer primaries have a yellow wing spot, and the inner ones have a white spot. The feet are a yellowish orange; the bill is yellow and gray at the base. The female resembles the male but has less yellow on the head, and the ceres and beard area are black. *Requirements:* Gold-crested grackles that are kept singly soon become friendly, but they are happier living in pairs in an aviary. However, matching a pair is difficult because these birds are available so irregularly at pet stores. Otherwise, their needs are like those of mynahs. *Voice:* Varied calls and whistling, similar to the utterances of mynahs.

(The remainder of this chapter was written by Matthew M. Vriends, Ph.D.)

The Thraupidae Family (Tangers)

Tanagers are still considered to actually belong to the finch family (Fringillidae) by ornithologists.

These birds very seldom eat seeds, however, and the majority of them have various types of fruits and berries as their main fare. Their favorite fruits include soaked, dried currants and raisins, grapes, cut pear and apple, dates, figs, bananas, and halved oranges. In addition, insects (cut mealworms), soaked coconut cookies, and finely shredded carrots are most welcome. Because of their basically sweet and juicy food, their droppings are watery. Consequently the bottom of cages and glass or show cages should be covered with absorbent paper towels or a few layers of newspaper or construction paper. Daily cleaning is essential to avoid diseases. Washing facilities in the cage or aviary must always be present and need to be cleaned and refilled with boiled and then cooled water a few times a day.

Successful breeding results in captivity occur only sporadically. To improve your chances, you should work with large aviaries. It is best to work with an aviary that is well stocked with greenery and houses just a few birds. (Incidentally, tanagers have a fairly good relationship with Pekin robins; see page 24.) They prefer to breed as high up as possible in a variety of nesting boxes already containing nesting material in the form of coconut fibers, dead and live grass, leaves, moss, pieces of bark, wool, and the like. Quite often they also choose to build their nest by themselves in a spot picked in a shrub of some sort (select thick shrubs for the aviary). It is a good idea, however, to place in the bushes a few "nest shells" made of chicken wire bent into the shape of a little bowl — but watch out for sharp edges! It is a shame that virtually all the imported birds are males.

If you do succeed in breeding tanagers, you must watch out that the parents do not aggressively pursue their young once they are independent. Both independent offspring and fellow species are best removed from the aviary, particularly when the parent birds start on a new brood. The young tanagers are considered independent after about 20 days, at which time you should catch them and remove them from the aviary to avoid unpleasantness. Young birds can achieve true coloring after

Description of Popular Softbills

about 1 year, but some species may take as long as 1½ years.

Recently imported birds should be kept where a temperature of 77°F (25°C) can be maintained; this temperature can be gradually dropped to 68°F (20°C) after acclimation.

Hobbyists in the United States should remember that possession of native North American tanagers is against U.S. federal law, so these species should not be collected or purchased through a black market.

Superb Tanager
(Also known as orange-rumped or seven-colored tanager.)
Tangara fastuosa (Lesson, 1831)

Distribution: Eastern Brazil in Pernambuco and Alagoas. *Habitat:* This species prefers to live in small groups in forests in hilly country. They spend their time high up in the crowns of trees, leaving only when they seek food. *Overall length:* 5½ inches (14 cm). *Appearance:* The male is velvety black around the beak, the forehead and chin, the center of the throat, and the upper back; the lower back and rump are orange, as are the three outermost secondaries of the wings. The head and neck are covered with scaly, glossy green-blue feathers. The band that separates the chin and throat is also silvery green-blue. Flight and tail feathers are black

with dark blue-purple edges and red tips. Lesser wing coverts are greenish blue. Underwing coverts are grayish black. The underside is dark purple-blue, lighter on the chest. The rest of the body is black. The eyes are brown, the beak is black, and the feet are dark brown. The female has a greenish blue head, but the rest of her coloring is less vivid, with the back being more green and dull orange-yellow (the male is darker yellow with orange). The plumage of juvenile birds is duller before the first molt and does not have the gloss of the adult male. *Behavior:* This species is very inquisitive and becomes tame rapidly. Nevertheless, I would strongly advise you to allow them to breed only when kept in a well-planted aviary where there are no small exotic birds; it occasionally happens that they steal eggs or young birds out of the nests of small finches and waxbills. Large birds can respond aggressively when necessary to protect their eggs and their young, so it is fairly safe to keep this species together with several varieties of somewhat larger aviary birds. However, even under these circumstances, caution and vigilence are strongly recommended.

Requirements in captivity
This tolerant bird is regularly offered for sale and prefers a high proportion of insects in its daily diet. The bird should be kept at a constant temperature of 77°F (25°C), although this temperature can be gradually decreased to 68°F (20°C) after proper acclimatization.

Breeding Data
Nesting sites in nature: In bushes and other dense cover. Cup-shaped nest.
Incubation and nestling care: The hen does most of the incubation, but male and female take turns feeding the nestlings.
Clutch: Two to four pinkish red, almost fully marked eggs. Size of eggs: 20 × 10 mm.
Incubation period: 13 to 14 days.
Nestling period: 12 to 14 days.

Description of Popular Softbills

Related Species

Blue-breasted Tanager

(Also known as green-headed tanager.)
Tangara seledon (P. L. S. Mueller, 1776)

Distribution: Southeastern Brazil, eastern Paraguay, and northeastern Argentina. *Habitat:* These birds prefer to live in the mountains, where they virtually play hide-and-seek among rock crevices and cavities. They prefer to live in small groups, and on warm, sunny afternoons they perch in the highest treetops they can find to enjoy the sun. *Overall length:* 5½ inches (14 cm). *Appearance and disposition:* Essentially similar to the preceding species. The male has a narrow black band above the upper mandible and a purple-green head with a light blue sheen. There is a black border along the bottom of the cheeks and quite a bit of green bordering the black band of the lower mandible, with some black mixed in. The chest is silvery blue. Shoulders, back (partly interrupted by black), and rump are yellow, changing to green. Wing coverts are black with green edges, the lesser wing coverts purple. The underside is grass green. The eyes are brown, the bill is black, and the feet brown-black. The entire body of the female is less vivid in color. *Requirements in captivity:* Daily spraying and refreshing bathwater kept at room temperature must not be forgotten. Apart from the large variety of fruit, you should also offer a mixture of rusk crumbs, ant pupae, small mealworms, grated carrots, and heart, followed by finely chopped egg. Finely chopped red meat (with any fat trimmed off first!) is also very welcome. These beautiful birds can be kept in a roomy cage or, better, in a well-planted aviary. If kept in a cage, the bottom needs to be covered daily (never with sand!). Offer shell sand in a separate dish. Since the birds consume a lot of fruit, their droppings are usually thin. The paper covering the bottom of the cage has to be changed regularly to prevent infestation with disease-carrying bacteria.

The Ramphastidae Family (Toucans)

Toucans stand out because of their huge bills. The toucan's bill is, however, very light because it is made of hollow bone cells. Only the edges of the bill are hard and serrated. It is also strange that toucans completely lack "beard" feathers. These birds have long, narrow tongues that are frayed at the edges. The area around the eyes is unfeathered. Toucans' wings are short and rounded, and the tail is also rounded. The birds walk very poorly because their first and fourth toes are directed backward. There are about 60 species in tropical America. Because the early German ornithologist Schomburg reported that the giant toucan or toco toucan ate Spanish peppers, this family inherited the name pepperbirds, but these days they are generally only known by the name of toucans.

Mr. Clive Roots states the following: "They are gregarious birds and often when one is shot by hunters the other members of the group respond to the cries of the wounded bird and mob the hunter."

Toucans love to bathe frequently. They need thick perches for both sitting and sleeping; these should have a diameter of about 2½ inches (6½ cm).

Toco Toucan

(Also known as giant toucan.)
Ramphastos toco (Mueller, 1779)

Distribution: Eastern South America from the Guianas to northern Argentina. This species is very sociable and likes to roam in noisy small flocks through the upper levels of the forest, searching for fruits, eggs, young birds, and reptiles. *Overall length:* 19½ inches (48 cm). This species is the largest toucan. *Appearance and disposition:* The sexes look alike; both are black with a white rump, throat, and foreneck. The undertail coverts are red. The eyes are dark blue, the bill is orange-yellow with a black spot at the tip of the upper mandible, and the feet are blue-gray. *Requirements in captivity:* The

species likes to use the highest branches for perching. Recently imported birds often suffer from damaged or infected eyes as they have the habit of constantly jabbing at each other while in the shipping crates. Adults caught in the wild, which for some reason must be force-fed, seldom survive such treatment and, according to Roots, are best placed in a warm room, provided with water and a wide choice of food, and left completely alone. Consult an avian veterinarian immediately. The diet is made up of fruits of all kinds (sultanas, soaked raisins and currants, dried figs, oranges, pears, apples, bananas, and grapes; the last five should be diced). Mealworms and various other insects are gladly accepted as well as some raw red meat; an occasional dead mouse should be provided.

This species needs a high flight; it is pointless to provide a planted aviary since the bird destroys the plants in no time at all. Supply strong branches, placed high in the aviary.

Breeding Data

Nesting sites in nature: In a tree hole.
Incubation and nestling care: By both sexes.
Clutch: 2 to 4 white eggs.
Incubation Period: 16 to 18 days.
Nestling period: About 6 to 7 weeks.

Useful Literature and Addresses

Axelson, R. Dean: *Caring For Your Pet Bird*, Blandford Press/Sterling, New York, 1984

Von Frisch, Otto: *Mynah Birds*, Barron's, New York, 1986

Gallerstein, G. A.: *Bird Owner's Home Health and Care Handbook*, Howell Book House, Inc., New York, 1984

Gerstenfeld, Sheldon L.: *The Bird Care Book*, Addison-Wesley, Reading, Massachusetts, 1981

Roots, Clive: *Softbilled Birds*, Arco, New York, 1970

Rutgers, A. and Norris, K. A.: *Encyclopedia of Aviculture*, Blandford Press, Poole, Dorset, England, 1972

Vince, Colin: *Keeping Softbilled Birds*, Stanley Paul, London, England, 1980

Vriends, M. M.: *Simon & Schuster's Guide to Pet Birds,* Simon & Schuster, New York, 1984

— *The Macdonald Encyclopedia of Cage and Aviary Birds*, Macdonald & Co., London, England, 1985

Periodicals

A.F.A. Watchbird, The (Bimonthly; American Federation of Aviculture, P.O. Box. 1568, Redondo Beach, CA 90278)

American Cage Bird Magazine (Monthly; One Glamore Court, Smithtown, New York, 11787)

Avicultural Bulletin (Monthly; Avicultural Society of America, Inc., P.O. Box 2796, Dept. CB, Redondo Beach, CA 90278)

Avicultural Magazine (Quarterly; The Avicultural Society, Windsor, Forest Stud, Mill Ride, Ascot, Berkshire, England)

Cage and Aviary Birds (Weekly; Prospect House, 9–15 Ewell Road, Cheam, Sutton, Surrey, SM3, 8BZ, England); young birdkeepers under 16 may like to join the Junior Bird League; full details can be obtained from the J.B.L., c/o *Cage and Aviary Birds*

American Bird Clubs

American Federation of Aviculture, Inc. (see *The A.F.A. Watchbird*)

Avicultural Society of America (see *Avicultural Bulletin*)

Australian Bird Clubs

Avicultural Society of Australia, c/o Mr. I. C. L. Jackson, Box 130 Broadford, Victoria, 3658

Avicultural Society of Queensland, 19 Fahey's Road, Albany Creek, Queensland, 4035

Canadian Bird Clubs

Avicultural Advancement Council, P.O. Box 5126, Postal Station "B", Victoria, British Columbia, V8R 6N4

British Columbia Avicultural Society, c/o Mr. Paul Prior, 11784-90th Avenue, North Delta, British Columbia, V4C 3H6

Calgary and District Avicultural Society, c/o Mr. Richard Kary, 7728 Bowcliffe Cr., N.W., Calgary, Alberta, T3B 2S5

English Bird Club

The Avicultural Society (see *Avicultural Magazine*)

New Zealand Bird Club

The Avicultural Society of New Zealand, Inc., P.O. Box 21403, Henderson, Auckland 8

Veterinarian Association

Association of Avian Veterinarians, P.O. Box 299, East Northport, New York, 11731

Bringing Birds into the USA

What Is a Pet Bird?

A pet bird is defined as any bird, except poultry, intended for the personal pleasure of its individual owner, not for resale. Poultry, even if kept as pets, are imported under separate rules and quarantined at USDA animal import centers. Birds classified as poultry include chickens, turkeys, pheasants, partridge, ducks, geese, swans, doves, peafowl, and similar avian species.

Importing a Pet Bird

Special rules for bringing a pet bird into the United States (from all countries but Canada):
- USDA quarantine
- Quarantine space reservation
- Fee in advance
- Foreign health certificate
- Final shipping arrangements
- Two-bird limit

If you're bringing your pet bird into the country, you must:

Quarantine your bird (or birds) for at least 30 days in a USDA-operated import facility at one of nine ports of entry. The bird, which must be caged when you bring it in, will be transferred to a special isolation cage at the import facility.

Reserve quarantine space for the bird. A bird without a reservation will be accepted only if space is available. If none exists, this bird either will be refused entry or be transported, at your expense, to another entry port where there is space.

Pay the USDA an advance fee of $40 to be applied to the cost of quarantine services and necessary tests and examinations. Currently, quarantine costs are expected to average $80 for one bird or $100 per isolation cage if more than one bird is put in a cage. These charges may change without notice. You may also have to pay private companies for brokerage and transportation services to move the bird from the port of entry to the USDA import facility.

Obtain a health certificate in the nation of the bird's origin. This is a certificate signed by a national government veterinarian stating that the bird has been examined, shows no evidence of communicable disease, and is being exported in accordance with the laws of that country. The certificate must be signed within 30 days of the time the birds arrive in the United States. If not in English, it must be translated at your cost.

Arrange for shipping the bird to its final destination when it is released from quarantine. A list of brokers for each of the nine ports of entry may be requested from USDA port veterinarians at the time quarantine space is reserved. (See addresses to follow.) Most brokers offer transportation services from entry port to final destination.

Bring no more than two psittacine birds (parrots, parakeets, and other hookbills) per family into the United States during any single year. Larger groups of these birds are imported under separate rules for commercial shipment of birds.

Ports of Entry for Personally Owned Pet Birds

Listed below are the nine ports of entry for personally owned pet birds. To reserve quarantine space for your bird, write to the port veterinarian at the city where you'll be arriving and request Form 17-23. Return the completed form, together with a check or money order (contact the veterinarian in charge of the import facility for current costs) made payable to the USDA, to the same address. The balance of the fee will be due before the bird is released from quarantine.

Port Veterinarian
Animal and Plant Health Inspection Service (APHIS)
U.S. Department of Agriculture
(City, State, Zip Code)
New York, New York 11430
Miami, Florida 33152
Laredo, Texas 78040
El Paso, Texas 79902

Bringing Birds into the USA

Nogales, Arizona 85621
San Ysidro, California 92073
Los Angeles, California (Mailing address, Lawndale, CA 90261)
Honolulu, Hawaii 96850

The Quarantine Period

During quarantine, pet birds will be kept in individually controlled isolation cages to prevent any infection from spreading. Psittacine or hook-billed birds will be identified with a leg band. They will be fed a medicated feed as required by the U.S. Public Health Service to prevent psittacosis, a flulike disease transmissible to humans. Food and water will be readily available to the birds. Young, immature birds needing daily hand-feeding cannot be accepted because removing them from the isolation cage for feeding would interrupt the 30-day quarantine. During the quarantine, APHIS veterinarians will test the birds to make certain they are free of any communicable disease of poultry. Infected birds will be refused entry; at the owner's option they will either be returned to the country of origin (at the owner's expense) or humanely destroyed.

Special Exceptions

No government quarantine (and therefore no advance reservations or fees) and no foreign health certificate are required for:
• U.S. birds taken out of the country if special arrangements are made in advance. Before leaving the United States, you must get a health certificate for the bird from a veterinarian accredited by the USDA and make certain it is identified with a tattoo or numbered leg band. The health certificate, with this identification on it, must be presented at the time of re-entry. While out of the country, you must keep your pet bird separate from other birds. Remember that only two psittacine or hookbilled birds per family per year may enter the United States. Birds returning to the United States may come in through any one of the nine ports of entry listed earlier. There are also certain other specified ports of entry for these birds, depending upon the time of arrival and other factors. Contact APHIS officials for information on this prior to leaving the country.
• Birds from Canada. Pet birds may enter the United States from Canada on your signed statement that they have been in your possession for at least 90 days, were kept separate from other birds during the period, and are healthy. As with other countries, only two psittacine birds per family per year may enter the United States from Canada. Birds must be inspected by an APHIS veterinarian at designated ports of entry for land, air, and ocean shipments. These ports are subject to change, so for current information, contact APHIS/USDA officials.

Pet birds from Canada are not quarantined because Canada's animal disease control and eradication programs and import rules are similar to those of the United States.

Other U.S. Agencies Involved with Bird Imports

In addition to the U.S. Public Health Service requirement mentioned earlier, U.S. Department of the Interior rules require an inspection by one of its officials to assure that an imported bird is not in the rare or endangered species category, is not an illegally imported migratory bird, and is not an agricultural pest or injurious to humans. For details from these agencies, contact:

Division of Law Enforcement,
Fish and Wildlife Service,
U.S. Department of the Interior,
Washington, D.C. 20240

Bureau of Epidemiology,
Quarantine Division,
Center for Disease Control,
U.S. Public Health Service,
Atlanta, Georgia 30333

Bringing Birds into the USA

U.S. Customs Service,
Department of the Treasury,
Washington, D.C. 20229

For additional information on USDA-APHIS regulations, contact,

Import-Export Staff,
Veterinary Services, APHIS,
U.S. Department of Agriculture,
Hyattsville, Maryland 20782

Two Serious Threats to Birds

As a bird owner, you should know the symptoms of exotic Newcastle disease, the devastating disease of poultry and other birds mentioned elsewhere. If your birds show signs of incoordination and breathing difficulties — or if there should be any unusual die-off among them — contact your local veterinarian or animal health official immediately. Place dead birds in plastic bags, and refrigerate them for submittal to a diagnostic laboratory. Keep in mind that this disease is highly contagious, and you should isolate any newly purchased birds for at least 30 days. Although exotic Newcastle disease is not a general health hazard, it can cause minor eye infection in humans.

If you're tempted to buy a bird you suspect may have been smuggled into the United States, don't! Smuggled birds are a persistent threat to the health of pet birds and poultry flocks in this country. Indications are that many recent outbreaks of exotic Newcastle disease were caused by birds entering the United States illegally. If you have information about the possibility of smuggled birds, report it to any U.S. Customs office or call APHIS at Hyattsville, Maryland, (301) 436-8061.

Index

(Numbers in *italics* indicate color photographs; C1, front cover; C2, inside front cover; C3, inside back cover; C4, back cover)

Index

Index

Japanese white-eye, 81
Jerdon's leafbird, 84

Keratin, excessive, 59

Lamprospreo superbus, *17*, 91
Lamprotornis splendidus, *17*, 91
Leafbird, 80, 81–84
Leaf mold, 36
Leg bands, 53
Leiothrix argentauris, *28*, 70–71
Leiothrix argentauris laurinus, *28*, 71
Leiothrix lutea, *27*, 68–70
Lesser mealworm, 40
Life expectancy, 67
Lighting, 21
Live food, 35–36
    See also Growing live food
Luring, 64

Maggot, 44
Mail-order dealers, 9
Mating, 49
Mating season, 49
Mealworm, 39–40
Medicine cabinet, 55
Milk, 35
Milk products, 35
Mixed species, 24
Molds, 61
Molt, 63
    abnormal, 59–60
    caused by fright, 63
Moniliasis, 61
Muscicapidae family, 71–75
Mutual preening, 65–66
Mynah, *C4*, *17*, 88–90
Mynah pellets, 35

Natural branches, 14
Nectar dispenser, 15
Nectar drink, 33–34
Nest box, 48
Nest building, 48
Nesting basket, 48
Nesting material, 48
Nestling period, 50–51
Nest location, 49

Newcastle disease, 99
New quarters, 22
Nictitating membrane, 64
Niltava sundara, *45*, 75
Nutrition, state of, 10

Orange-bellied leafbird, *80*, 84
Orange-rumped tanager, 93
Oriental white-eye, *C2*, 76–78, 81
Osteomalacia, 61
Outdoor aviary, 16, 19–21
    wintering in, 26

Pagoda mynah, *C3*, 91
Pair, 7, 65
Pair bond, 66
Pair formation, 49
Parasites, 60–61
Pekin robin, *C1*, *27*, 68–70
Perch, 14–15
Periodicals, 9, 96
Pesticides, 39
Pet bird, 97
Pet dealers, 9
Pets, 7
Pigment, feather, 63
Plumage, 10
Poisoning, 61
Pollen, 35
Ports of entry, 97–98
Potworm, 43
Preening, mutual, 65–66
Preventive medicine, 54
Prey, catching, 35–36
Proximal vane, 62
Pycnonotidae family, 84–87
Pycnonotus cafer, *79*, 87
Pycnonotus capensis, *79*, 87
Pycnonotus jocosus, *79*, 85–87
Pycnonotus leucogenys, *79*, 87

Quarantine, 97
    cage, 54
    exceptions to, 98
    period, 98

Rachis, 62
Ramphastidae family, 94–95
Ramphastos toco, 94–95

Ready-to-eat food, 33
Rearing, 51
Red-eared bulbul, *79*, 85–87
Red mite, 60-61
Red silver-eared mesia, *28*, 71
Red-vented bulbul, *79*, 87
Respiratory system problems, 57
Rickets, 61
Rod, 62
Roundworm, 60
Routine maintenance, 25
Rufous-bellied niltava, *45*, 75

Same species, 24
Seeds, 35
Sensory organs, 64
Seven-colored tanager, 93
Shama, *46*, 71–74
Shower, 25
Sick bird, 9–10
Sickness. See Health care
Silver-eared mesia, *C4*, *28*, 70–71
Singing, 64–65
Singing lessons, 23-24
Single bird, 7, 23
Siva cyanouroptera, *27*, 71
Sleeping, 66
Smell, sense of, 64
Smuggling, 99
Snowy-headed robin chat, 74–75
Social behavior, 65-66
Softbill:
    buying advice, 9–10
    characteristics of, 8
    and children, 7
    keeping, 6–7
    and pets, 7
    singles vs pairs, 7
    vacation care, 7
Splendid glossy starling, *17*, 91
Staggers, 58
Starling, 87–92
Structural color, 63
Sturnidae family, 87–92
Submission gesture, 65
Sunbathing, 25
Superb glossy starling, 91
Superb tanager, 93
Supplemental foods, 35

102

Index

Syrinx, 64

Tanager, 92–94
Tangara fastuosa, 93
Tangara seledon, 94
Tapeworm, 60
Taste, sense of, 64
Temenuchus pagodarum, 91
Tenebrio molitor, 39
Terrarium cage, 13
Thraupidae family, 92–94
Threadworm, 60
Thrush, 61
Timaliidae family, 68--71

Toco toucan, 94–95
Tonki bulbul, 87
Toucan, 94–95
Trip home, 22
Trust, building, 23

USDA, 97

Vacation care, 7
Veterinarian trip, 56–57

Walking stick, 41–42
Water dish, 15
Wax moth, 43

White-eared bulbul, *79*, 87
White-eye, 76–78, 81
Winter care, 25–26
Wire cage, 12
Worming, 55

Yeast infection, 61
Yellow-headed leafbird, 84

Zosteropidae family, 76–78, 81
Zosterops erythropleurus, *18*, 81
Zosterops japonicus, 81
Zosterops palpebrosus, 76–78, 81

"A solid bet for first-time pet owners"
—Booklist

We've taken all the best features of our popular Pet Owner's Manuals and added *more* expert advice, *more* sparkling color photographs, *more* fascinating behavioral insights, and fact-filled profiles on the leading breeds. Indispensable references for pet owners, ideal for people who want to compare breeds before choosing a pet. Over 120 illustrations per book – 55 to 60 in full color!

"Stunning"
– Roger Caras
Pets & Wildlife

Ulrike Müller
The New Cat Handbook

Includes a Special Section on Cat "Language" and Behavior

Choosing a Cat • Care & Feeding • Health • Breeding • Showing

• Data on All Major Breeds • 130 Color Photos and Drawings

BARRON'S

Hans-J. Ullmann
The New Dog Handbook

Choosing a Dog • Training • Care & Feeding • Health • Understanding Dogs

• Data on 60 Breeds and 130 Color Photos and Drawings

BARRON'S

The New Saltwater Aquarium Handbook

Setting up a Marine Aquarium • Selecting Fish and Invertebrates • Aquarium Maintenance • Disease Control • Nutrition

• Over 60 Full-Color Photos

BARRON'S

THE NEW AQUARIUM HANDBOOK, Scheurmann (3682-4)
THE NEW AUSTRALIAN PARAKEET HANDBOOK, Vriends (4739-7)
THE NEW BIRD HANDBOOK, Vriends (4157-7)
THE NEW CANARY HANDBOOK, Vriends (4879-2)
THE NEW CAT HANDBOOK, Müller (2922-4)
THE NEW CHAMELEONS HANDBOOK, Le Berre (1805-2)
THE NEW COCKATIEL HANDBOOK, Vriends (4201-8)
THE NEW DOG HANDBOOK, H.J. Ullmann (2857-0)
THE NEW DUCK HANDBOOK, Raethel (4088-0)
THE NEW FINCH HANDBOOK, Koepff (2859-7)
THE NEW GOAT HANDBOOK, Jaudas (4090-2)
THE NEW PARAKEET HANDBOOK, Birmelin / Wolter (2985-2)
THE NEW PARROT HANDBOOK, Lantermann (3729-4)
THE NEW RABBIT HANDBOOK, Vriends-Parent (4202-6)
THE NEW SALTWATER AQUARIUM HANDBOOK, Blasiola (4482-7)
THE NEW SOFTBILL HANDBOOK, W. Steinigeweg (4075-9)
THE NEW TERRIER HANDBOOK, Kern (3951-3)

Barron's Educational Series, Inc.
250 Wireless Blvd., Hauppauge, NY 11788
In Canada: Georgetown Book Warehouse
34 Armstrong Ave., Georgetown, Ont. L7G 4R9
Barron's ISBN prefix: 0-8120   (#63) R3/96
Order from your favorite bookstore or pet shop.

BARRON'S